The County Palatine and Bishoprick of Durham, drawn by Saxton; corrected and amended with additions by P. Lea, 1686.

A HISTORY OF COUNTY DURHAM

Durham knocker

A History of County Durham

D. POCOCK and R. NORRIS

Cartography and Illustrations by
Steven Allan, Arthur Corner,
David Cowton and David Hume

PHILLIMORE

1990

Published by
PHILLIMORE & CO. LTD.
Shopwyke Hall, Chichester, Sussex

© Douglas Pocock and Roger Norris, 1990

ISBN 0 85033 714 3

Printed and bound in Great Britain by
BIDDLES LTD.
Guildford, Surrey

Contents

Badge of Bishop Richard Fox (1494-1501)

List of Maps

*St Mary's church,
Staindrop*

List of Plates

*Coat of arms, Bishop
Thomas Wolsey
(1523-28)*

Acknowledgements

The authors acknowledge the following sources and wish to thank the following for permission to use photographs: D.C.D. Pocock (front cover and nos. 1,3,5,7,10,13,14,18,19,20,48); A.F. Harding and R. Young, *Durham Archaeological Journal*, 2, 1986 (no. 2); Department of Archaeology, University of Durham (no. 4); The Librarian, University of Durham, Cosin MS. v. 11.6, f. 77v, (no. 8); Beamish, The North of England Open Air Museum, County Durham (nos. 9,22,23,36-39 inclusive, and back cover); D. Hudspeth (nos. 11 and 12); T. Allom (nos. 15 and 30); P. Nixon (nos. 16 and 17); T. Richmond (no. 21); Durham County Council, Environment Department (nos. 24,40, 41,44,49,50); *The Palmer Record*, III, 1905 and IV, 1907 (nos. 25 and 35); J.F.C. Morland, *L'Art d'exploiter les Mines de Charbon de Terre*, 1777 (no. 26); T. Hair, *Sketches of the Coal Mines in Northumberland and Durham*, 1844 (nos. 27 and 28); Borough of Darlington Museum (no. 29); the Librarian, Durham County Council (no. 31a); the Archivist, Durham County Council (no. 31b); Museums Officer, Borough of Hartlepool (no. 31c); City Librarian and Arts Officer, Newcastle upon Tyne (no. 31d); C. Bartram (no. 32); Sunderland Museum and Art Gallery, Tyne and Wear Museum Service (nos. 33 and 34); Durham Miners' Association (no. 42a); the Librarian, South Tyneside Borough Council (nos. 42b and 43); Editor, *Northern Architect*, 47, 1969 (no. 42c); English Estates (North) (no. 45); Commission for the New Towns, Washington (no. 46); British Coal, Newcastle upon Tyne (no. 47).

The maps were drafted by Douglas Pocock and professionally drawn by Arthur Corner, David Cowton, David Hume and Steven Allan of the Department of Geography, University of Durham. David Hume was responsible for many of the drawings. The photographic preparation was by Derek Hudspeth, assisted by Michelle Johnson. The manuscript was largely typed by Edith Pocock.

9

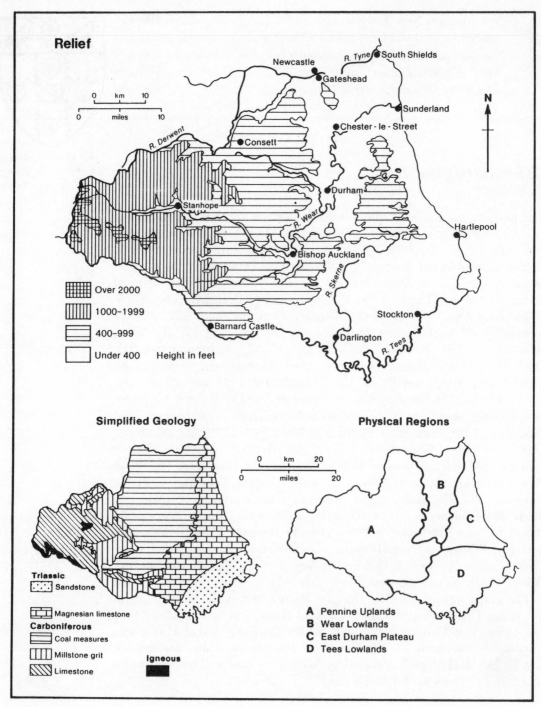

Relief

0 km 10
0 miles 10

N

R. Tyne
South Shields
Newcastle
Gateshead
Sunderland
Chester - le - Street
R. Derwent
Consett
Durham
Stanhope
Hartlepool
R. Wear
Bishop Auckland
R. Skerne
Stockton
Barnard Castle
Darlington
R. Tees

Over 2000
1000–1999
400–999
Under 400   Height in feet

Simplified Geology

0 km 20
0 miles 20

Triassic
Sandstone

Magnesian limestone
Carboniferous
Coal measures
Millstone grit
Limestone

Igneous

Physical Regions

B
C
A
D

A Pennine Uplands
B Wear Lowlands
C East Durham Plateau
D Tees Lowlands

Map 1. County Durham: relief, geology and physical divisions.

10

I The Setting

The stage on which the history of County Durham has been enacted forms a compact area of just over 1,000 square miles of north-eastern England. The rivers Tyne, with its tributary the Derwent, and Tees tidily delimit the area to the north and south, respectively. Westwards the county has its beginnings in the high Pennines in the backbone of England, at a unique anchor point which it shares with four other historic counties. It is from here, at Burnhope Seat some 2,450 ft. above sea level, that the county's own river, the Wear, begins its initially purposeful eastward journey to the sea. In mid-course, however, it changes character and meanders northwards, incorporating, as if in homage, a loop around the promontory of the cathedral city after which the county is named; it then surprisingly shuns an obvious confluence with the Tyne by turning east again to carve with difficulty its own mouth at Sunderland. An explanation for the behaviour of the Wear is embedded in the story of the physical evolution of the area. As a prologue to the history of the county, a brief outline of this physical background will enhance an appreciation of subsequent human response, for the former has set a variety of problems and questions, at the same time offering clues and opportunities for understanding the relationship between mankind and the environment.

The entire solid geology of the county is given a gentle eastwards dip by the anticlinal folding of the Pennines. The strata thus become progressively younger towards the coast, from Carboniferous, through Permian to Triassic in the south-east (Map 1). The western half of the county comprises the Pennine Uplands, a dissected plateau-like block of Carboniferous Limestone forming the highest moorlands, with broad ridges and fell tops continued eastwards by sandstone bands of Millstone Grit. A change in the bedrock to Lower Coal Measures below approximately the 1,000-ft. contour makes little initial difference to relief and appearance (blanket peat and heather). In the intervening dales igneous intrusions have affected the valleys of the upper Wear and Tees, most spectacularly in the waterfalls of Cauldron Snout and High Force where quartz-dolerite, part of the Whin Sill, occurs. The same series of intrusions is responsible for the deposits of vein minerals — lead, zinc, fluorite, barite and witherite.

High Force, Teesdale

11

Marsden Rock

The progressive eastward decline in altitude of the Coal Measures has been accentuated by the Wear in its central section, here flowing northwards at right angles to the original tilt of the land. Consequently, a Wear Lowlands region may be recognised, delimited roughly by the 400-ft. contour to the west but strongly to the east by the sharp rise of the Magnesian Limestone escarpment. The Lowlands have a rolling topography, a feature largely attributable to the variable distribution of glacial drift. Beneath the drift lies a considerable thickness of the so-called 'exposed' coalfield, a succession of sandstone, shale and clay bands, together with some ironstone, in addition to some twenty coal seams.

The prominent escarpment of Permian Magnesian Limestone, rising to 700 ft. in the south-west but lower to the north, is breached at only two points — by the river Wear to the north and by the Ferry Hill Gap in the south. The same escarpment, of course, marks the line at which the coalfield becomes 'concealed' beneath the Permian series. From the relatively level scarp top the gentle dip-slope of the Magnesian Limestone forms the East Durham Plateau which ends at the sea in a pronounced 50-100-ft. cliffline. North of Sunderland the cliff has been moulded into spectacular stacks, most notably at Marsden Rock. Here and there the coastline is cut by deeply-incised ravines or denes; the mouth of the Wear is cut into the plateau in similar manner.

The Triassic deposits which underlie the extreme south-east of the county are everywhere masked by a thick deposit of glacial drift. Even so, much of the Tees Lowlands is less than 100 ft. above sea level and has areas of poor natural drainage in a gently rolling landscape. The Skerne is the most notable of the left-bank tributaries of the Tees.

The foundation of solid geology, which itself has been subject to folding and faulting and cycles of erosion on a geological time scale — the oldest rocks were laid down some 250,000,000 years ago — was given much of its surface detail only during the last 30,000 years as a result of the most recent ice age. The advance and retreat, or build-up and stagnation, of over 1,000-ft. thickness of ice that covered the county brought a wide range of erosion and depositional effects. At one time a Scandinavian ice sheet mingled with that of advances originating in the Southern Uplands and Cheviots and in the Lake District. Upland features were sharpened, channels were cut by meltwater and a new topography was given to most of the area below 600 ft. with glacial or fluvio-glacial deposits of clays, sands and gravels. In the middle Wear Lowlands the superficial drift deposits may exceed 200 ft. in thickness. Notable deposits are the well-sorted sands and gravels which originated in a lake trapped between the Pennine foothills and Permian escarpment to west and east and by the retreating ice to the north. The prominent

12

Ferryhill Gap (265 ft. above sea level) represents a spectacular melt-water channel which allowed the trapped waters to drain southwards. To the north the ice-blockage contributed to the Wear being diverted in the vicinity of the present Chester-le-Street eastwards across the Permian escarpment. Its broad, truncated former valley, which continues to the Tyne, is today occupied by the Team, a stream hardly worthy to be called river. For the length of its present northward course the cross-profile of the middle Wear exhibits an alternating succession of wide, open valley and narrow gorge. The former result from the reworking of the superficial deposits and exhuming of former drift-filled channels; gorges occur where the downcutting, initiated on the same drift, encountered and cut into the buried solid geology. The incised meander loop around Durham City is the best-known example of a relatively widespread landscape feature.

The climatic amelioration, which led to the progressive retreat and disappearance of the ice sheet, allowed vegetation to colonise the surface of the newly-emergent and freshly-fashioned landscape. At first, from about 10-12,000 years ago, a covering of grasses and herbaceous plants spread north and west, to be followed by a succession of forest species — pine and birch, then hazel, elm and oak, with alder by 3,000 B.C. The same approximate date marks the first arrival of man as a significant environmental agent, although for perhaps the two preceding millennia a few small and scattered communities had hunted over parts of the area. A hunting and gathering economy only had a negligible effect on the environment, but the Neolithic era marked the beginnings of forest clearing and cultivation, thus initiating the sequence of landscape change which inexorably was to gain momentum over the centuries as the interplay of migrants and indigenous peoples affected settlement and colonisation, exploitation and development. The history of the county has thus been played out on a stage increasingly shaped by man himself. It is the aim of the succeeding chapters to highlight the significant strands that have gone into the weaving of the present tapestry.

II Prehistoric Durham

Mesolithic deer-horn harpoon, Whitburn

Although it is the longest time period in our survey, the prehistoric imprint can hardly be described as indelible. This stems not only from the subsequent erasing of any record or from lack of detection, but from the very location of the county. This meant that it was among the last to emerge from beneath the retreating ice cap and, later, when rising sea level severed Britain from the continent, among the most distant from the entry point of peoples into this country. The only surviving confirmed evidence from the Palaeolithic era or Old Stone Age, for instance, is the single palaeolith found at Warren House Gill situated on the (present-day) coast. The environment can hardly have been inviting to the few nomadic hunter-gatherers, for at the beginning of the period the mean annual temperature hovered around 0°C in a cold, dry 'continental' climate classified as Boreal, associated with which was a slowly encroaching tree cover of juniper, birch and, later, pine.

More evidence of man's activity is available from the following Mesolithic or Middle Stone Age. The gradual amelioration in climate resulted in an Atlantic phase which was both warmer — some 2-4°C above present day — and wetter. There was an accompanying spread of deciduous woodland, on which the technology of the hunter-gatherers could still make but little permanent impression. The predominant — and characteristic — implement was the microlith, flakes struck from a stone core and shaped accordingly. Relatively few axes from cores have been found. Although the county's only sources of workable stone were from drift deposits and beach pebbles, Filpoke Beacon in south-east Durham provides the country's earliest example of narrow-blade (Tardenoisian) culture, dating from the early seventh millennium. The overall distribution of finds, along the coast with a sprinkling inland near major river courses, could suggest seasonal migration by the colonisers. The distribution of over 50 polished axes from the succeeding Neolithic era reinforces the earlier pattern; a concentration along the Wear valley speaks of a commercial highway from a 'factory' working the Langdale volcanic tuffs in the Lake District (Map 2). This broad continuity suggests a transmission of the new culture among Neolithic peoples as much as large-scale immigration originating from the Rhinelands and Low Countries. What is not in doubt, however, is that the

Neolithic axe, Esh Winning

14

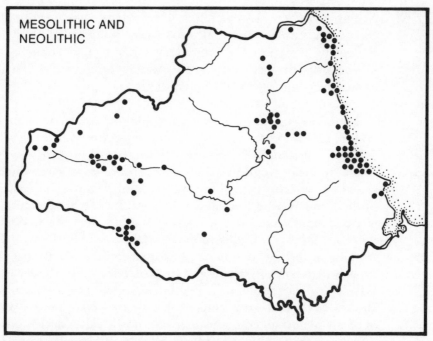

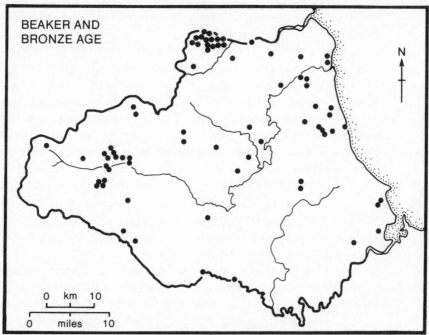

Map 2. (a) Mesolithic and Neolithic finds in County Durham; (b) Beaker and Bronze Age finds in County Durham. Substantial finds only are shown, giving a broad indication of the spread of early man in the county.

15

Beaker in cist burial,
Ryton

Neolithic era saw the beginning of woodland clearance for small-scale agriculture and early domestication, accompanied by the first permanent settlement as opposed to temporary shelters. This applies particularly to the better-drained soils on the Magnesian Limestone in the northeast of the county, where is found the Ireshopeburn long barrow, round cairns and round barrows.

Round cairns and barrows, containing burials in stone-lined cist graves, which began to appear at the beginning of the Neolithic era, became increasingly associated with short-neck beaker-like vessels after which the Beaker culture was named. Examples of such round barrows are those at Hastings Hill (Sunderland), Copt Hill (Houghton-le-Spring) and West Brandon. To the west, further architectural evidence of ritual significance are the standing stones and stone circles on Barningham Moor, Middleton-in-Teesdale and Hunstanworth. Metalworking in the new culture is illustrated in the early Bronze Age shield from Broonyholm peat bog and, impressively, from the Heathery Burn Cave site (near Stanhope). The latter, one of the most important late Bronze Age metal-work finds in the country, comprised a wide variety of weapons, ornaments and utensils (not least a sheet-bronze bucket) and the earliest known evidence of wheeled transport in Britain. A contemporary photograph shows a selection of these, many of which are now in the British Museum (Plate 2).

Agriculture had also firmly imprinted itself on the landscape by the end of the period, not least on the higher ground in the west of the county where activity was encouraged by the optimum post-glacial climate. A regular spacing of some half-dozen sites on the western slopes of the Upper Tees suggests that the area at this time was organised into a number of large farming units. Excavation of the substantial house and enclosure of one of them, Bracken Rigg, points to a mixed economy and permanent, rather than seasonal, occupation. Flints suggest hunting (and a continuation of Mesolithic techniques where bronze metallurgy was inferior), a spindle-whorl reflects woollen cloth making and animal husbandry, and pollen suggests small-scale cereal production. The enclosure could have been used for both arable and stock. Pottery urns were made from local boulder clay.

The subsequent climatic deterioration, which set in towards the end of the Bronze Age, led to the preservation of the colonising imprint on the Pennines as they were abandoned to become the peat and heather moorland which we know today. Beneath this later surface covering on Barningham Moor and Bracken Rigg, for instance, is preserved extensive evidence of the agricultural system and settlement — boundary banks, ditches and ploughing patterns, along with the foundations of circular stone dwellings.

Flint dagger,
Washington

16

An upturn in climate as the Iron Age (700 B.C.-A.D. 70) progressed encouraged a concentration of human effort for the first time in the naturally less well drained lowlands. Extensive woodland clearance occurred in the middle Wear valley and in the southern part of the county in the Tees lowland. Rectilinear or sub-rectangular enclosures containing one or more circular structures provide the characteristic feature of the farming people. Modern aerial photography has revealed an increasing number of ditches, gullies and hedgebanks of field systems, along with round houses and trackways. Thorpe Thewles, where house sites extend beyond the enclosure, is a well-recorded example in the Tees lowland. West Brandon, in the centre of the county, has the most spectacular round-house, with a single building 60 ft. in diameter within its ditched and palisaded enclosure. The substantial number of querns discovered in the county confirms the evidence of pollen analysis of widespread cereal cultivation, while at the same time cautioning against a simple interpretation of aerial photographs. In the Tees lowlands, for instance, the greater photographic detection of crop-marks on the lighter, gravel-based soils, compared with the heavier soils derived from boulder clay, could reflect the greater impressionability of the former soils as much as assumed pastoralism on the latter.

The rectangular enclosures of the Iron Age peoples were undefended settlements. Scattered among them on raised ground were a few defended sites, thus continuing the barrow-type settlement from the previous age. Maiden Castle (Durham) and Toft Hill (Bishop Auckland) are good examples. In general distribution as well as detailed siting, the barrows of both the Bronze and Iron Ages are related to major river valleys, located on eminences within, or on the edge of, the actual lowlands. A presumed cremation practice accounts for an absence of burials and, of course, any interred artefacts. Such defensive sites of a people constituting the northernmost grouping of the Brigantes (literally 'upland people') were, however, ignored by the succeeding Roman invaders. Different criteria were to determine their choice of military settlements.

III Roman Durham

Gold plate, dedicated to Mars, Lanchester

The date of the Roman invasion of England in A.D. 43 is well known, but it was a further three decades before their influence spread to the north-east and Durham became the northern border zone of the Empire. Lying to the south of the best known Roman monument in Britain, Hadrian's Wall (built A.D. 122-128), the county itself was lightly Romanised judged in terms of known monuments and artefacts. The major features are roads and associated forts.

Dere Street, constructed during the military governorship of Agricola (A.D. 78-84), is the earlier and more important of two north-south arteries. Entering the county at Piercebridge, it makes for Corbridge, over two days' march away in the vicinity of the Wall. Forts guarded the important artery at local river crossings — Piercebridge (Magis) being on the Tees, Binchester (Vinovia) by the Wear and Ebchester (Vindomora) by the Derwent (see Map 3). Forts and highway together are seen essentially as a joint instrument of consolidation. There is no evidence of hostile native populations, anyway, and only one tentatively identified site of campaigning — a possible marching camp near Lanchester. The evacuation of both Binchester and Ebchester for two decades in the middle of the second century, to be replaced by a single more centrally-positioned new fort at Lanchester (Longovicium), can be taken as further evidence of the area's stability. The re-occupation of the two vacated forts, together with the building of a new one at Chester-le-Street (Concangium) in the 160s, may be interpreted as part of a broader strategy whereby forts in the county provided auxiliary centres for troop concentration for expeditions north of the Wall.

The military settlement at South Shields (Arbeia) performed a distinctive role in the Romanising of the area, guarding the eastern flank of the Wall and serving as a port and supply base to the county and beyond. Pottery finds suggest an early wooden fort on the site as a base for Agricola's fleet, a role emphasised again when it was temporarily converted into a supply base for the campaigns of Emperor Septimus Severus into Scotland in the early third century. Its significance as a store base can be gauged from the size of its two dozen granaries which, it is estimated, would have been capable of serving an army of 10,000

Funeral monument to Regina, South Shields

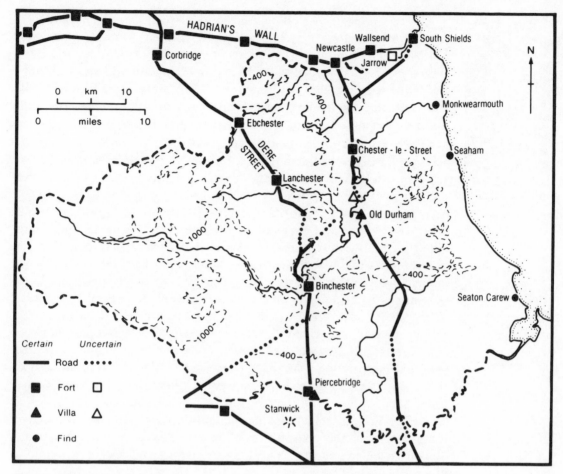

Map 3. Roman County Durham.

men for almost a year. (The total estimated garrison strength along the Wall was just under 10,000.) The fort itself, which had been reconstructed in stone by the middle of the second century and extended at the beginning of the third, was again rebuilt at the end of the same century, thereby emphasising its continuing garrison function. A recent imaginative on-site reconstruction of one of its gates provides a ready visual clue to the importance of this easternmost unit of the Wall system (Plate 3). It is logic rather than imagination, however, which links military inscriptions along with coins and pottery finds at Jarrow to suggest it was the site of another fort (or signal station), thus filling the gap between South Shields and Wallsend. Along the coast, discovery of middens or pottery similarly underlies the suggestion of a chain of signal stations at Monkwearmouth, Seaham and near Seaton Carew.

Altar to Aesculapius and Salus, Binchester

The two largest forts, Binchester and Piercebridge, have both presented problems for the archaeologist. The former, enclosing nine acres, has borne the intriguing attribution of Ptolemy as a city of the Brigantes. Since there is no evidence of pre-Roman settlement on the site, and since this is the sole reference to Brigantes in the county, the accuracy of the statement may be queried. Meanwhile, excavation of the deserted hill-top site has exposed the most perfectly preserved hypocaust in the North.

At Piercebridge excavations have revealed the ground plan of an 11-acre fort dating from the fourth century on the north bank of the Tees, adjacent to a civilian settlement, but, strangely, no evidence of an earlier military installation which is considered to have existed from the very beginning of Agricola's northern campaign. It is reasoned that it would have been foolhardy of an invading force, after plundering the important hillfort of Stanwick only three miles to the south-west in A.D. 71, not to have left a military presence at this strategic river crossing. An area immediately south of the river has yet to be confirmed as the site. Even evidence of the bridging of the Tees has come to light only fairly recently. In the 1930s oak piling was discovered in the river bed; in the 1970s stone piers were excavated 200 yards downstream. The former, predictable from the north-south alignment of Dere Street, is the presumed original bridge dating from the A.D. 90s. The latter, dated to the second century by finds on both shores, is located where the much lower banks would have allowed the river to spread laterally during its episodes of severe flooding, thereby reducing the build-up of potentially destructive water pressure; the constriction of flood water is presumed to have destroyed the higher crossing. The safer crossing point necessitated a diversion of Dere Street to the east (Plate 4).

While pottery finds show that the county's forts were occupied until at least the last quarter of the fourth century, all had attendant civilian settlements (*vici*) which, having been emergent market centres during the occupation, doubtless lingered when the Romans withdrew. There is, however, no evidence of a classical grid-pattern in their layout. Even Piercebridge, the largest, appears to have grown organically. Neither is there evidence that the classical urban lifestyle of the southern part of the country was replicated in the county. The virtual absence of villas reinforces this last point. Just to the south of Piercebridge, at Holme House, remains of a bath-house, mosaic pavements and a round house point to the existence of a true villa. Within the county there is just Old Durham, where a fourth-century bath-house is assumed to have been once associated with a main building subsequently lost in gravel quarrying, and the suggestion of a possible second site at Finchale. The latter two can be seen to be located in relation to Cade Road, which, being

Statuette, ploughman and aratrum, Piercebridge

20

the later of the two north-south arteries, was constructed for administrative and commercial, rather than military purposes. The sole fort on the road from Middleton St George on the Tees to the bridge on the Tyne at Newcastle (Pons Aelius) was the later garrison of Chester-le-Street.

Beyond the features outlined, there is little to denote any further distinct material imprint by the colonising Romans. Iron Age culture persisted, forest clearance intensified and cereal cultivation rapidly became widespread over the central and eastern parts of the county in a climate comparable to the present day. The area surrounding Bishop Middleham was noted for its hemp cultivation. Parts of the west of the county were used for the hunting of deer and boar, not least by Roman officers seeking a sporting diversion, judging by inscriptions on elaborate altars found at Eastgate and Stanhope. Lack of other obvious evidence, not least of a road in Weardale, may puzzle historians, but then, it is not unusual for the quest for historical tidiness to be thwarted, albeit temporarily.

Altar to Silvanus,
Stanhope

IV   The Early Middle Ages and County Durham

The Early Middle Ages, between the departure of the Romans and the arrival of the Normans, saw the replacement of a British or Romano-British world by an English one, through a series of invasions by Teutonic peoples from the northern shores of Germany and Scandinavia. Much remains uncertain concerning what we popularly call the Dark Ages, but certainly long before the end of the six centuries it was possible to recognise the foundations of a distinctive unit that had emerged between the Tyne and the Tees, between the kingdoms of Bernicia and Deira, centred on Bamburgh and York, respectively. Within the emergent county area the basic features of rural settlement were also recognisable and the site of the future county town had been chosen as the final resting place for the North Country's most famous saint.

The invasion of the North-East by Angles or Anglo-Saxons from the northern coast of Germany or Denmark, which began in earnest under King Ida in the mid-sixth century from his Bamburgh bridgehead, was consolidated by Aedelfrith (593-617) through battlefield victories over the native Celtic and Scottish tribes and through marriage into the royal house of Deira. The united houses formed an extensive kingdom between the Humber and Forth, which for a century was the country's largest and most powerful unit. Associated with political stability was a christianising of the area and a blossoming of monasticism, the latter hosting a renaissance of learning when, for a period, Northumbria was the intellectual centre of Europe.

The conversion of the pagan Anglo-Saxons, effected by a Celtic missionary movement which came through lowland Scotland, illustrates the fusion between native and invading peoples. It was King Oswald, converted while in exile in Scotland, who brought Celtic monks from Iona to found a monastery at Lindisfarne under Aidan in 635. In this same act can be traced the spiritual and ecclesiastical roots of Durham, for it was the episcopal seat associated with Lindisfarne that was eventually and eventfully transferred to Durham. South of the Tyne there was a second religious foundation of high significance. A monastery had been founded at Hartlepool under St Hilda in 647, but it was the twin monasteries of Monkwearmouth (Sunderland, 674) and Jarrow (681), founded by Benedict Biscop at the request of Northumbrian king Ecgfrith, which were to influence history (Plates 5 and 6).

St Peter's, Monkwearmouth, and St Paul's, Jarrow, were 'Roman' foundations, following in the wake of the momentous Synod of Whitby in 664 at which it was decided that the country's church organisation and practice would follow the continental or Roman method, rather than the Celtic. This fusion of Celtic and Anglo-Saxon cultures in contact with the continental church led to more than the dissemination of the Roman rite and calendar. Craftsmen reintroduced the arts of stone masonry, brick and tile manufacture and glazing, including stained-glass windows. The small stained-glass windows at Jarrow are considered the oldest, not only in this country but in Europe, for although glaziers were brought from Gaul no evidence of their craft on the continent remains. (Roman glass was colourless.) From their several visits to Rome Benedict Biscop and Bishop Wilfred brought back not only relics but also pictures and books for the twin monasteries. The well-stocked libraries, containing the greatest collection of manuscripts in the country, were the stimulus for the production and copying of a large number of texts, many for missionary work throughout Anglo-Saxon England, in Scotland, Ireland and the continent. The best-known of its distinctively illustrated manuscripts is the great Bible known as *Codex Amiatinus*, a copy of which was dispatched in 716 as an offering to the Pope. The 1,550 calf-hides for vellum which were required to produce this volume are an indication of the monastery's scale and wealth. If the Lindisfarne scriptorium is accorded the greater artistic achievement, most notably in the *Lindisfarne Gospels*, the joint foundation of St Peter and St Paul was the acknowledged centre of intellectual creativity. Its most famous scholar was Bede (674-735), born nearby at Monkton, who spent his life from the age of seven in the Jarrow monastery. Biblical scholar, historian and grammarian, the 'venerable' Bede is acknowledged as the 'father of English learning'. His *Ecclesiastical History of the English Church and People* provided this country with a unique record of its early evolution, thereby helping to foster a national identity among the Anglo-Saxon peoples. A measure of the value of the work, produced seven centuries before the aid of printing, is that some 160 medieval copies still survive.

Beyond the monastic world, an ecclesiastical organisation for the whole area began to take shape. The initial divisions were extensive, served by one church or 'minster'. Early possible sites for centrally-located minsters were Chester-le-Street, Lanchester, Billingham, Sockburn and Gainford. Free-standing carved stone crosses provided sup-

*Anglo-Saxon cross,
St Andrew, Auckland*

plementary nodes or gathering points for worship, and possibly burial, before the broad network was subdivided to create the beginning of a parochial system. The crosses which have survived have been incorporated within churches, as in St Andrew's, Auckland. A collection of them has been assembled in the Monks' Dormitory in Durham Cathedral.

The age of monasticism ended abruptly. In 794, a year after the first Viking raid on Lindisfarne, Jarrow was attacked and both it and Monkwearmouth were eventually abandoned. They presumably presented accessible sites to any seaborne attack, undefended and full of transportable valuables. The secular state of Northumbria was now in poor shape to offer effective defence, having been weakened by border warfare against hostile Picts, Britons and Mercians, by its internal succession feuds and, ironically, because of the previous generosity of converted kings who endowed the Church rather than rewarding aristocracy — thus weakening the state's power base. However, invasion, as opposed to piracy, by the Scandinavian Vikings — mainly from Denmark — did not occur for another 70 years and came overland from the south. After landing in East Anglia and advancing to York, Halfdan led an expedition northwards in 874 and easily took the Northumbrian kingdom. Monasticism and church organisation were destroyed, and earls of Bamburgh henceforth had but restricted powers. An effective authority, secular as well as religious, came to be attached to the peripatetic Community of St Cuthbert, which, having left Lindisfarne in 875, eventually settled for over a century at Chester-le-Street in 882. An event of considerable significance occurred the next year, when Bishop Eadred of the Community lobbied successfully for the elevation of Guthred to the vacant throne in York. In return, the new king granted undisputed retention of extensive estates between the Tyne and Wear, which were formerly held by the monasteries of Monkwearmouth and Jarrow, and allowed the purchase of estates in the eastern and southern half of the county (Map 4a). In being given right of sanctuary and customs in all lands north of the Tees, the bishop and his successors became the king's patron and protector: in other words, the palatinate authority of the bishopric was born.

Danish settlement rather than conquest did not generally extend north of the Tees, except in the southern part of the county where place-names, and to a lesser extent sculptural remains, provide supporting evidence (Map 4b). Around Sadberge (Old Danish for 'flat hill') immigrants were sufficiently numerous for the hundred or ward to be called a wapentake. West and east of the wapentake, as far as Barnard Castle and Hartlepool respectively, place-names suggest the implanting of Danish settlements between sites already occupied. The place-name suffixes *-by* (village) and *-thorpe* (hamlet) are the most numerous. The

*Pectoral cross,
St Cuthbert*

24

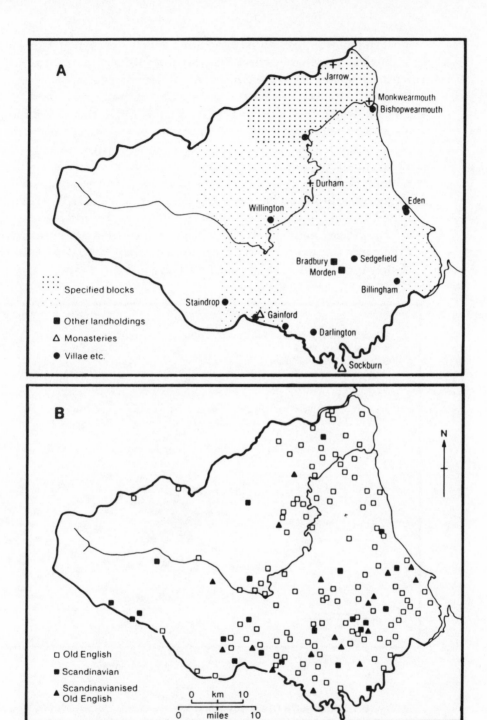

Map 4. (a) Lands and settlements belonging to St Cuthbert Community, late ninth century; (b) the distribution of Old English or Anglo-Saxon and Scandinavian place names.

25

most common suffixes of the earlier and widely distributed Anglo-Saxon or English place-names are *-ham* (homestead), *-ton* (farmstead), *-worth* (enclosure) and *-wich* (also enclosure). Relative frequency of occurrence, however, cannot be equated exactly with original colonisation. Village sites of British or Celtic origin (Auckland, Egglescliffe, Penshore, for instance) must have been more numerous than is suggested by the few place-names that have survived. A few Romano-British settlements were given Anglo-Saxon form — Great Stainton, Ebchester, Lanchester, for example. Interestingly there was less take-over of ancient names relating to natural features. The major rivers, Tyne, Tees and Wear, all bear British names, as do most of the main tributaries. Hybrid names suggest a compromise, most notably in the instance of the settlement that was to give its name to the county: Durham is derived from *Dunholm*, a hybrid of the Anglian *dun* (a hill) and Old Danish *holmr* (island).

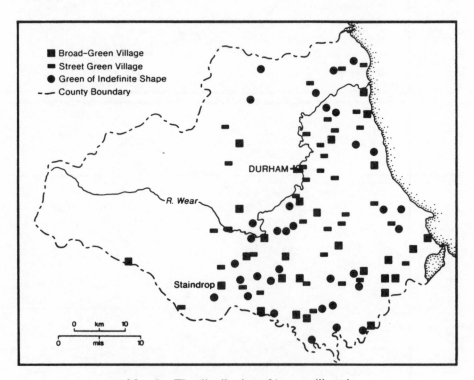

Map 5. The distribution of 'green villages'.

Whatever the settlement place-name, its characteristic form was nucleated, with homesteads clustered around a central green. Some hundred so-called 'green villages' have been recognised, mainly to the south and east of the Wear, that is, in that part of the county most suitable for agriculture. Originally offering a defensive role, the enclosed green was also used as pasture. Markets were held on the more important ones. The greens were most often aligned west-east, and varied in size, perhaps enclosing several acres. Their shape was used by Harry Thorpe in his classification of Durham's green villages (Map 5, and Plates 9 and 10); Brian Roberts has more recently included other morphological features in a more detailed categorisation.

Among the settlements, Durham was confirmed in its key role in our story in 995 when the Community of St Cuthbert, no longer feeling safe at Chester-le-Street, journeyed south as far as Ripon before returning with the coffin of St Cuthbert and other precious relics to the 'hill island'. (The wanderings of the Community and the dead saint's part in choosing his final resting-place are recorded in Sir Walter Scott's poem, *Marmion*.) With the site chosen, Aldhun, last bishop of Chester-le-Street, now first bishop of Durham, induced his son-in-law and future earl of Northumbria, Uchtred, to impress the population between the rivers Tees and Coquet to build a shrine worthy to contain the North Country's greatest saint. Over 20 years of effort saw the rise of a twin-towered stone building of suitable magnificence to outshine any previous construction. The architectural context in which it arose can be judged from the modest dozen or so Saxon churches which have survived to the present day — from the simple nave and chancel construction, without tower (Escomb, Seaham) or with tower (Jarrow, Monkwearmouth), to a cruciform type, with crossing tower (Norton). Magnificence notwithstanding, the renowned 'White Church', as it was known, was destined to disappear within the century as part of a new beginning ushered in by the next wave of invaders.

Carving on the side of St Cuthbert's coffin

V   County Durham in the Middle Ages

Pillar capital, Durham Castle

It was from the consolidation of his rule after the Battle of Hastings in 1066 that King William I gained the title Conqueror. A national revolt broke out in 1068 when the advent of the fleet of Sweyn of Denmark in the river Humber encouraged Edgar the Aetheling, who had taken refuge in the court of King Malcolm III of Scotland, to invade Northumbria. In 1069 the Conqueror sent Robert Cumin with 700 men northward to take control of Northumbria. The cruelty of Cumin was well-known and on 31 January the local population fell upon him and his men billeted in Durham City. Cumin was burned to death in his lodgings and only one of his followers escaped to tell the tale. King William's vengeance was swift and the demise of the last Saxon bishop of Durham, Aethelwin, saw the election of Walcher of Lorraine as the first Norman bishop in 1071. The building of the King's castle at Durham commenced, first the motte and then the keep. After the execution of Waltheof in 1076, Bishop Walcher was given the title of Earl of Northumbria.

In 1093 a new cathedral of locally-quarried sandstone, to replace the Saxon 'White Church', was begun by the second Norman bishop, William of St Calais. Even more than the castle, the cathedral was a massive show of Norman imperial power — 'half castle 'gainst the Scot', in Sir Walter Scott's memorable phrase. Its construction was also architecturally significant in that it incorporated for the first time in Europe high-ribbed vaulting for its roof, supported by concealed buttresses. The building's prime function was to house the shrine of St Cuthbert, in whose name the cathedral was dedicated. The pace of building was impressive.

Between 24 and 29 August 1104 the new basilica received the body of the patron St Cuthbert in the presence of Turgot the prior, Bishop Rannulph Flambard and a great assembly. Simeon the Chronicler records that the brethren asserted the body of St Cuthbert still to be incorrupt, so, perhaps understandably, there was a demand that this should be generally proved. Therefore the shrine and coffin were opened and the abbot of Séez was entrusted to show that the body of the hermit-saint was whole. The abbot moved the limbs and apparently convinced those present. So the remains of the saint were settled behind the high

28

1. Teesdale, looking west up the Tees, between Eggleston and Middleton-in-Teesdale.

2. Heathery Burn hoard of late Bronze Age artefacts.

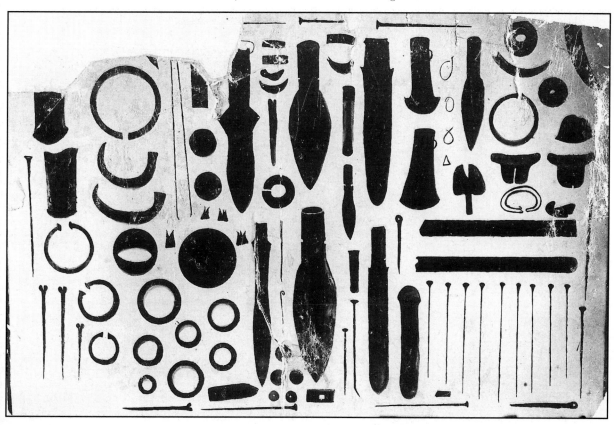

3. Excavated Roman military settlement of Arbeia, South Shields, with the recent reconstruction of the West Gate.

4. Roman Piercebridge, looking south. The site of the military fort is occupied by the modern village, and the civil settlement can be traced in the adjacent field. The exposed stone piers leading to the former bridge are on the far left.

5. St Paul's church, Jarrow, with Saxon tower and chancel. Ruins of the monastic buildings are in the foreground.

6. St Peter's church, Monkwearmouth, also a former monastery, with Saxon tower.

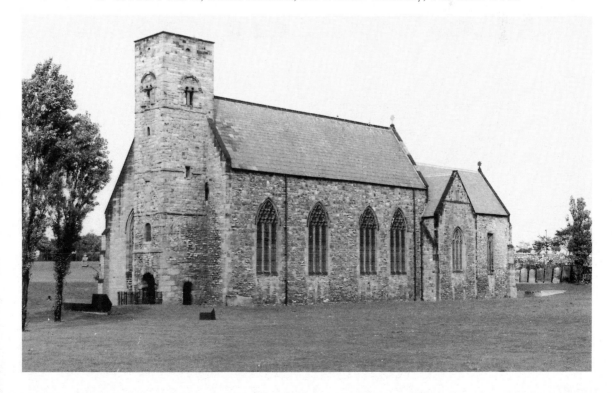

7. St John's church, Escomb, near Bishop Auckland, dating from the seventh century and largely built with Roman stone from Binchester.

8. Part of *Historia Dunelmensis Ecclesiae* (1104) by Symeon, a monk of Durham. It refers to the appointment of William of St Carilef as bishop in 1081.

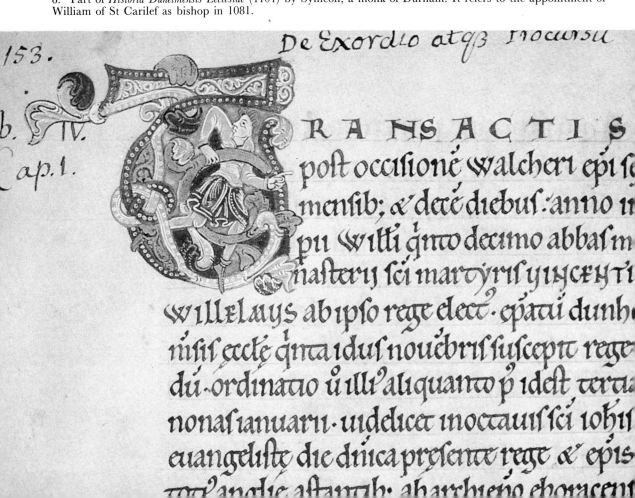

altar in the cathedral to be a focus for the affection of the inhabitants of County Durham. The shrine became a centre of pilgrimage in England rivalling that of St Thomas à Becket in Canterbury.

William of St Calais was responsible not only for having planned and set in motion the construction of a mighty cathedral. A transfer of sovereign power, justifying or consolidating the term 'prince bishop', can also be attributed to him, for in 1093 St Calais was granted a charter by William Rufus allowing him to hold in free alms all those lands in England for which he had previously owed military service to the crown. St Calais, a frequent advisor to the king, was certainly one of the most eminent personages in both Church and State in Norman England.

Durham became a frontier county against the Scots when, in 1136, King David I of Scotland invaded England in support of his niece, the Empress Maud, pretender to the English throne. King David took Norham Castle in Northumberland and progressed with his army as far as Durham. When King Stephen came to Durham in February 1137 he forced the Scottish king to retire to Newcastle and Norham was given up to the English under peace terms. There was a renewed assault from Scotland in 1138 and Norham was besieged. Geoffrey Rufus, bishop of Durham, remained loyal to King Stephen and unavailable to the blandishments of the Scottish king who, failing to capture Wark, advanced south with his army. Although supported by Eustace FitzJohn, King David was defeated at the Battle of the Standard at Northallerton by Thurston, archbishop of York, and his forces on 22 August. A peace was concluded in which Henry, son of King David, was granted the earldom of Northumberland, though without any claim to the territory of St Cuthbert.

In 1141 King David took advantage of the mortal illness of Bishop Geoffrey to further the cause of his chancellor, William Cumin, to be elected bishop of Durham. The monastic electors proved intractable and on 14 March 1143 William of St Barbara was elected. Cumin conducted himself as if he were bishop, with all accompanying ecclesiastical and secular authority, and it was not until 18 October 1144 that Bishop William of St Barbara, with the help of the local barons, Roger Conyers, Geoffrey Escolland and Bertram Bulmer, was able to confirm his position. The intervening period was occupied by secular and warlike manoeuvres.

The consolidation of the powers and extent of the County Palatine was effected by Hugh of Le Puiset whose election as bishop of Durham in February 1153 kindled the resentment of the archdiocese of York. Hugh, in his mid-twenties and already much honoured, was King Stephen's nephew. He had been chosen by the monastic electors of Durham Abbey without the consent of the Metropolitan, Henry Murdac.

Episcopal seal, Bishop Hugh le Puiset

29

Geoffrey of Coldingham, the medieval chronicler, charged Hugh with being a dissembler and a hypocrite, but it is significant that King Henry II, on his accession in 1154, did not attempt to compel the dismantling of County Durham's fortified castles which had been a source of tumult in the previous reign. Rather he confirmed the liberties and privileges of the Palatinate: *'Deo et Sancto Cuthberto et ecclesiae Dunelm. et Hugoni epo. et omnibus successoribus suis quietas et liberas et imperpetuum'*. (For God and St Cuthbert and the continued peace and freedom of the Church at Durham and Bishop Hugh and all his successors.)

Hugh manipulated the intermittent strife between Scotland and England to his own advantage and the enhancement of his authority, permitting the Scots army under King William the Lion to pass through the county after the failure of the siege of Wark Castle in 1173. As great offices of state came to him, he achieved increasing secular authority and provided a large contingent to assist King Richard I in the Crusade of 1189. His preparations for the expedition were splendid; he had levied funds and had taken the cross as the sign of his intention to conquer the infidel. But his pride was disturbed when the king appointed him a regent to stay at home and maintain the realm, appropriating the collected taxes which were more use than Hugh's personal service in the conflict ahead.

These circumstances, though, provided an opportunity for Hugh to purchase the wapentake (an area similar to a hundred in the southern counties) of Sadberge on the north bank of the river Tees for £11,000. Included in the bargain were the Lordships of Hartlepool and Barnard Castle, together with — for Hugh's lifetime — the earldom of Northumberland. It is from this event that the unusual addition of a peer's coronet to the armorials of the See of Durham derives. The See already had the region north to the river Tyne and west to the river Derwent. It was a great estate.

To consolidate his property rights, and in so doing to fill a large gap in national records, Hugh ordered an account to be made of his estate in about 1180. The King's Commissioners, who had compiled *Domesday Book* 100 years previously, had not assessed Durham and Northumberland for tax obligations. The new survey listed, by holding, customary dues of money and labour owed to the bishop as a temporal lord of the see of St Cuthbert. The text gives the date 1183 and the first substantial entry is for the settlement of Boldon (just south of Jarrow). Hence the survey's familiar title, *Boldon Book*. Boldon was stated to contain 22 villeins, each having 30 acres (enough land to use two plough teams of eight oxen each year) and owing labour to the bishop of three days a week. Further dues of eggs, poultry, grain and wood were imposed, with four days' work at harvest for the whole household except the wife. Pairs

St Mary's church, Whickham

30

of villeins also had to build a booth at St Cuthbert's Fair in Durham City. The entry for Boldon provided a model for other communities — *'sicut villani de Boldon'* often occurs — and a clockwise perambulation of settlements in County Durham was observed before the survey entered Northumberland.

The *Boldon Book* gives a good impression of the early economy of the Bishopric. To the north a mixed economy of grain and cattle farming prevailed, with grain in the south-east. King Stephen had given permission for Bishop Hugh to mine lead in Weardale allowing him also to extract any silver therefrom. Iron and coal were mined in the west, timber cut and venison obtained in the Forest of Weardale. High quality coal was being won for the bishop by the end of the 14th century from Whickham and Gateshead which, being on the river Tyne, provided ease of transportation.

Estates held by the cathedral priory of Durham were not included in the survey. In 1083 the community which had grown and established itself around the shrine of St Cuthbert at Durham was replaced, at the behest of Bishop William of St Calais and with papal permission, by monks from the recently (1074) refounded Benedictine house at Jarrow. The prior and convent of Durham grew apart in power and authority from their titular abbot, the bishop. By the end of the 13th century the monastic income was over £2,000, and the Benedictine Community had over 100 brethren including those at the dependent houses at Jarrow, Wearmouth and Holy Island.

The establishment of a great monastic house at Durham and the power of the bishop throughout the county set the whole area apart, separate even from central government. The bishop was a great feudal and temporal lord who had courts of his own and his own chancellor to initiate actions therein. (The Chancery court of the County Palatine of Durham was only abolished in 1975, though by that time it was a purely secular jurisdiction with which bishops were no longer associated.)

Anthony Bek, bishop of Durham (1284-1310), Lord (Dominus) of (the Isle of) Man and Patriarch of Jerusalem, strengthened and increased the princely power claimed by his predecessors. A soldier and officer of state, he supported the campaign of King Edward I in 1296 when John Balliol, Edward's vassal King of Scotland, forfeited his throne for refusing to attend the parliament at Newcastle, and in 1298 he led a wing of the English army at the Battle of Falkirk, where William Wallace was defeated. Any pretensions of the archbishop of York to a right of visitation were disputed continually by Bek, and he had greedy eyes on the estates and privileges of the prior and convent of Durham. Bek was also a bold politician, and when Ralph Neville and John

St Cuthbert's church, Darlington

31

Norman pillars, St Lawrence's, Pittington

Marmaduke contested the right of the king to call on men of the Palatinate to do military service outside its borders, the bishop supported them against Edward. Later, he was not slow, however, to invest himself with the forfeited estates of Barnard Castle, Hart and Hartlepool.

The bishops meanwhile proceeded to fund collegiate churches at St Andrew, Auckland (South Church), Norton, Darlington, Lanchester and Chester-le-Street, which provided lucrative incomes for prebendaries (or canons) there as well as opportunities for scholarly work. A further collegiate church was founded in 1410 by the Neville family at Staindrop where Lord Barnard is still lay rector. Bishop Richard de Bury is probably the best-known scholar bishop of the Middle Ages; his tract, *Philobiblon*, 'On the Love of Books', has a timeless charm. The monastic regime at Durham included scholarship, writing and teaching. A monastic college was established at Oxford — Durham College, which after the dissolution was refounded as Trinity College. The cathedral's own teaching of novice monks and the opportunity provided for the chaplains of the 15th-century chantry of Bishop Thomas Langley to teach poor children has been continued in Durham School and Durham Chorister School.

Two hospitals from the Middle Ages still survive as flourishing, working and charitable bodies today. Bishop Hugh of Le Puiset founded Sherburn Hospital near Durham, in about 1181 when leprosy was prevalent in Europe, to care for 65 sufferers and also probably to care for pilgrims on their way to Durham. Bishop Robert Stichill founded Greatham Hospital in the south-east of the county in 1273 for 40 brethren — *ad infirmorum et pauperum inopiis providendum*. A further hospital had been founded in 1112 by Bishop Rannulph Flambard at Kepier (one mile north of Durham) where the gatehouse building still stands.

The bishops also improved ease of passage, particularly for pilgrims, by the provision of bridges, tolls from which could be used towards their repair. The building of Framwellgate Bridge in Durham City was traditionally associated with Bishop Flambard. Elvet Bridge took the road south from Durham and was built by Bishop Hugh of Le Puiset. Both bridges had to be restored and altered by Bishop Richard Fox in the late 15th century. Yarm, Croft and Winston bridges provided access into the county from the south. (The old tenure sword, the 14th-century Conyers Falchion was, until the middle of the 19th century, presented to a new bishop of Durham as he entered the county across the river Tees at Croft, a ceremony revived for David Jenkins in 1984.) The medieval Tyne Bridge, replacing the old Roman bridge in the mid-13th century — Matthew Paris the historian records the Newcastle upon Tyne fire of 1248 — was the joint responsibility of Newcastle upon Tyne Corporation and of the bishops of Durham. The Corporation's case to

Seal, Durham School

32

have authority over the whole was finally defeated at law in 1416 when Bishop Thomas Langley established his right to the southern third. Demarcation was indicated by two 'St Cuthbert's stones' built into the bridge.

Coat of arms of Bishop Thomas Langley (1406-37)

In general, community life of the county grew rapidly during this period, with improvements and maintenance of roads and bridges, although the corporate powers of the towns were kept in rein by the vigilance of the bishops. Markets prospered at Durham (charter of 1179-80), at Darlington, Barnard Castle, Hartlepool, Stockton, Sedgefield and Staindrop, and in Weardale at Wolsingham. Leland, though, in his itinerary of 1540, records that 'Woulsingham market, in Weredale, is clean decayed, for none repayre thither with ware or intayle on the consuete day'. Trade was organised in Durham City through guilds: skinners (1327), grocers (1345), mercers (1393), salters (1394), weavers (1450), cordwainers (1458), barber-surgeons (1468), butchers (1520), carpenters (1530), plumbers (1532), barkers and tanners (c.1540) and drapers (1549). Eight of these guilds have survived into the 20th century.

The stability of the county and its local communities had prospered as the danger from northern incursions faded. In October 1346, however, in the early years of the Hundred Years War and a couple of months after the Battle of Crécy, the Scots army under King David II invaded, taking advantage of the absence of King Edward III in France. The result was that King David was captured and his army routed by the English under Ralph Lord Neville, his son John, and Lord Percy, and 'by the mediation of holy St Cuthbert'. A western suburb of Durham City is named after the site of the battle — Neville's Cross. The emblems of victory, the banners of Ralph and King David, and the Black Rood from Edinburgh (a Scots national talisman), were ceremoniously set up near St Cuthbert's shrine in Durham Cathedral.

The Black Death, the 'prima pestilentia', which ravaged the Palatinate from 1349 to 1350, during the episcopate of Thomas Hatfield, was particularly violent in south-east Durham. It left the peasants ruined and disheartened, and gave the *coup de grâce* to the old system of serfdom and labour rents. Stewards found themselves unable to let the land at anything but a paltry rent. Often holdings were untilled and villages were abandoned. Tenants became insubordinate and, despite fines, were reluctant to accept wages at the level customary in 1347 as laid down in the statute of 1351. The authority of the Halmote Court (landlord and tenant) was increasingly disregarded and the sense of community holding within a vill was less of a binding force.

Through the influence of the Durham branch of the Neville family, Lords of Brancepeth and Raby castles and with great possessions in the western half of the county, Durham was a Lancastrian stronghold during

Neville's Cross, 1346

33

the Wars of the Roses. Surprisingly, during this period the county was free of conflict other than the continuing struggle to uphold the rights of the Palatinate. Thomas Langley, bishop for over thirty years, disputed the authority of a Commission from the King's Chancery to take an inquest at Hartlepool, and the bishop's princely rights between Tyne and Wear were confirmed by Parliament.

In 1477 Richard, Duke of Gloucester, took possession of Barnard Castle, which became one of his favourite residences. Three years later he was appointed commander-in-chief of the northern forces against the Scots, and became popular in the Palatinate, while Henry, Duke of Richmond, was appointed the king's Lieutenant-General north of the river Trent in 1522. Thus were the seeds sown for the development of the Council of the North and the dissipation of Palatinate powers.

Badge of Bishop Richard Fox (1494-1501)

VI Sixteenth- and Seventeenth-Century County Durham

The Jurisdiction of Liberties Act of 1536 had wiped away those privileges which had accrued to the office of Bishop of Durham, that is of appointing sheriffs, coroners and judges, collecting taxes, minting palatinate coinage, and administering civil and criminal law. Ecclesiastical privilege was seen by the monarch to be as insidiously dangerous as the growth of the great estates of the grandees of the county, the Neville, Lumley, Hylton and Eure families.

Seal of County Sheriff, 14th century

Although citizens of the area continued to use the courts of the bishop for legal redress, and the chancery of the bishop continued to issue writs, a significant break had occurred in the management of the bishopric. Justice was now seen to be done in the name of the monarch, and the bishops, beginning with Cuthbert Tunstall, gradually ceased to protect their medieval rights. Nonetheless disputes relating to the apportionment of offices great and small continued between the bishops and the great families into the 19th century. The 16th century saw the growth of the gentry class.

The year 1536 also saw the reaction to Thomas Cromwell, the Vicar-General of King Henry VIII who had lately assumed the title of Supreme Head of the Church of England by the Act of Supremacy of 1534. Cromwell's Machiavellian regime of fear intimidated clergy and nobility alike, and they feared, quite rightly, the threatening changes to their lives and institutions. The major county families, Nevilles, Hyltons, Lumleys, Bowes and Tempests, all played their part in joining the Pilgrimage of Grace, a remarkable movement of disaffection which encompassed the whole of northern England. The followers of this particularly demanded a re-union with the church of Rome and, in Durham, the restoration of the 'liberties' of the Palatinate. Only the Eures stood aside. Thirty thousand rebels moved on to Pontefract in Yorkshire where a Parliament of the North conceded the demands of the insurgents. The rebels disbanded. A further rising in January 1537 provided King Henry VIII with a pretext for ruthless and widespread repression, and Roger Lumley was executed for treason. Every concession was withdrawn.

Coat of arms of Bishop Cuthbert Tunstall (1530-59)

*Embroidered silk in
St Cuthbert's coffin*

The Visitation of the Monasteries in 1536 saw the attrition of the power of Durham monastery. In the cathedral the Commissioners of King Henry VIII, Doctors Lee and Henley and Master Blythman, defaced the shrines of St Cuthbert and the Venerable Bede. Behind the high altar in the area of the major shrine of St Cuthbert they had found 'many woorthie and goodly jewels . . . which by the estimate of those 3 visitors and their skilfull lapidaries that was of value sufficient to redeme a prince'. Remarkably, the near contemporary account of the last days of the monastery and also its customs and buildings, *Rites of Durham*, records that the Commissioners found the body of the seventh-century hermit saint from the Farnes incorrupt. It is related that '[Henley] did command them to take [the body of St Cuthbert] down, and so it happened contrary to their expectation that not only his body was whole and incorrupted, but the vestment wherein his body lay and wherewithall he was accustomed to say mass, was fresh, safe, and not consumed'. Saints and relics were in disrepute and subject to disrespect at the time, but a residual fear of the miraculous survived in the most hardened and sceptical of hearts.

The monastic establishment at Durham was surrendered to the King on 31 December 1539. The last prior of the old monastery and the first Dean (12 May 1541) were one and the same, Hugh Whitehead; 12 former monks became the first prebendaries or residentiary canons. The new age at Durham came in smoothly through the Reformation zeal of two succeeding deans, Robert Horne and William Whittingham, whose periods of office saw the understandable, though relatively modest, attempts to erase the religious features of the cathedral's old regime. Images were broken up and we read in *Rites* that the banner of St Cuthbert, which had been a symbol at the battles of Neville's Cross and Flodden, 'fell into the possession of one Dean Whittingham whose wife called Katherine . . . did most injuriously burn and consume the same in her fire in the notable contempt and disgrace of all ancient and goodly relics'.

Disaffection, and nostalgia for what had passed, led to the Northern Rising of 1569 — incited by the presence in prison at Tutbury in Staffordshire of Mary, Queen of Scots. Charles Neville, sixth Earl of Westmorland, who had married into the Roman Catholic Howard family, was her ally. In the autumn of 1569 Westmorland together with Thomas Percy, Earl of Northumberland, led a force from Raby Castle, near Staindrop, to Durham. The new Bibles printed in English were defaced and the old Mass was restored at the cathedral. The two earls had been in communication with the Spanish Ambassador, and the rebel forces held Hartlepool to keep open a passage from the continent. When Queen Mary was moved south to Coventry the rebels attempted to hold

Durham knocker

36

the North. The countryside as a whole favoured the rising, and in mid-November 1569 the two earls proceeded from Brancepeth to Barnard Castle, which was held by Sir George Bowes, loyal to Queen Elizabeth. Sir George, with an insufficient and arguably unreliable garrison, was under great pressure: '. . . very hard dyett and great want of bread, drynck and water; which was our only drynck, save I myxed yt with some wyne. I fownde the people in the castle in continuall mutenyes, seaking . . . to leape the walls and run to the rebells . . . I could hold no longer' — and he surrendered. But Alnwick and Warkworth castles had submitted to the loyal Sir John Forster and Sir Henry Percy. On 15 December, at a skirmish at Chester Dene to the north of Durham City, the two rebel earls were beaten, fleeing to Hexham. Charles Neville was attainted in 1571 and his estates in Durham forfeited to the crown, rather than to the bishop. The reason given was that the crown had had the business of defending them. Raby Castle remained crown property until 1645 when it was bought by the Vane family which later, by alliance with the Tempests, emerged as a major coal-owner. Thomas Percy was executed at York, the castles of Durham and Hartlepool were garrisoned, and over three hundred people were executed throughout the Palatinate.

Deer shelter, Auckland Park

Throughout the 16th century landlord-tenant conflict was common. During a time when prices were rising rapidly it was in the interest of the tenant to contest any attempt to increase rents. The great landlords, the Bishop of Durham and the Dean and Chapter, and the leading county families were, in the climate of the times, anxious to appear compassionate and not to act as rackrenters. Lesser gentry and yeomanry found opportunities to enhance their wealth by this holding-down of rents; they also achieved increasing influence by joining the bureaucracy which administered the county. The power of the old families decreased and the prerogatives of the bishops were challenged. The lively tenants of the bishop's Weardale estates disputed the judgement against them of the bishop's chancery court in 1620. They threatened to petition parliament for their case to be heard outside the county. They were concerned that their copyholds by inheritance at fixed rents or fines, or customary tenures, were in danger of attrition to tenancies at will — where a lease might be granted to someone other than the customary heir. Tenant right was protected under Common Law after a further agitation in 1639, this time by the tenants of the Dean and Chapter. The leaders of this campaign, later influential Parliamentarians, were George Grey, a coal-owner of Southwick, and Anthony Smith, a Durham lawyer.

Though County Durham continued to be predominantly a society whose economy was based on land and agriculture, lead-mining developed in the uplands of Teesdale, Weardale and Derwentside, and

37

coal-mining along the rivers Tyne and Wear. Newcastle and Sunderland were the great harbours which received the coal transported in keels from the riverside staiths at each colliery. The agricultural landscape at Whickham and Gateshead was transformed by pit-shafts. In 1589 Robert Bowes of Biddick started the production of sea-salt at Sunderland, an industry which also grew at South Shields. Bowes also owned collieries at Offerton. Other Wearside entrepreneurial coal-mining families were the Lumleys, the Lambtons, the Hedworths of Harraton and the Bellasises of Morton. At the beginning of the 17th century Sunderland hardly rivalled Newcastle as an exporter of coal. During the Civil War, however, when Newcastle was a Royalist stronghold, shipments of coal increased four-fold, and the area was dominated by the Parliamentarian families of Lilburne, Fenwick and Haselrigg.

Although Durham saw considerable action in August 1640 during the Bishops' War, after which part of the successful Scottish army was billeted on the county for nearly a year, it was not until January 1644 that the full impact of the Civil War was felt. Durham was the battlefield when Lord Leven's troops crossed the Tweed. He entered Sunderland, a parliamentarian borough, on 4 March and took South Shields on the 20th, thus commanding the entrances to the rivers Tyne and Wear and controlling ship-borne supplies. Montrose made some keen efforts to reverse the order of things and South Shields fort was recaptured in May. It was only a temporary respite, for by 27 July Newcastle, the last royalist bastion in the North, had fallen and the Scottish army was quartered in County Durham until February 1647.

Much privation and destruction was suffered. In 1640 the Council of the North was abolished by Act of Parliament, to be followed in 1646 by the bishopric and its privileges, and in 1648 by the Dean and Chapter of Durham. Plague broke out in 1644; horse-racing was forbidden at Auckland and Woodham. After the Act of 1646 episcopal property was put up for sale, and among the many beneficiaries the most successful was Sir Arthur Haselrigg. He bought the manor of Bishop Auckland, including the ancient palace of the bishops, for a little over £6,000. Stockton Castle, another refuge of the bishops, was demolished in 1652, and after the Battle of Dunbar, in September 1650, about three thousand of the defeated Scots prisoners were incarcerated in Durham Cathedral where they caused as much damage as had been done at the Reformation. The Neville chantry tombs were spoiled and the surviving portion of the medieval great paschal candlestick was stolen.

Durham City corporation seal, 1606

It was not until 1654-6 that the county was enfranchised for the first time, and then only temporarily, because of the Civil War. In April 1642 the Parliament in London had passed a bill that permitted Durham County and Durham City to elect two representatives each. Until that time the County Palatine, that is the Bishop of Durham, was the County's only representative in Parliament, with the continued right of being a justice of the peace. Parliament had taxed Durham in 1610. Sir Edwin Sandys, the contemporary advocate of constitutional monarchy, quite rightly argued that the people of County Durham should not 'be governed by laws whereunto they be no parties'. Although some protested that it was the county's traditional 'privilege' not to send members to Parliament, the moves for representation grew, and the bishop of the time, William James, felt threatened. Prominent amongst those in favour of the change were the coal-owners, and this was seen in some quarters as an attempt to create trouble for the ecclesiastical magnates, the Bishop and the Dean and Chapter, and to undermine their prerogatives. At the time of change in 1642 proposals to enlarge the franchise to give members specifically for Barnard Castle and Hartlepool were thrown out. With the restoration of the monarchy and the election of John Cosin to the See of Durham, it was stated that representation threatened the bishop's 'power and prerogative'. The county was not properly enfranchised until February 1672/73 after Cosin had died and before Lord Crewe had been translated to the see. The rightful grievance of freeholders and tenants was at last resolved.

Arms of Bishop John Cosin (1660-72)

John Cosin may seem obscurantist in respect of his care for his rights, but he was a man of great influence both nationally and locally. He restored the magnificent chapel at Auckland Castle and parts of the castle at Durham, and mid-17th-century ornate woodwork in churches in the county is often due to his encouragement. He endowed almshouses at Bishop Auckland and Durham, and reintroduced elaborate and stately worship with ornaments and music which had been the subject of much litigation in the 1620s and 1630s when Cosin was a canon at Durham. Motive notwithstanding, the princely building of Cosin would not have been possible without the resumed opulence of the bishopric. The Reformation may have reduced the power, but it was to be another two centuries before the line of 'golden bishops' yielded to a redistribution of revenues in a second Reformation of the 1830s.

The latter half of the 17th century saw County Durham housing ecclesiastics of the first order of learning. In 1657, during the Commonwealth, letters patent had been issued in response to a succession of petitions from the inhabitants of County Durham to establish a college, school or academy for the Northern Counties in Durham. Philip Hunton, author of *Treatise concerning Monarchy*, was appointed first Provost of Durham College. Unfortunately, the College did not survive the Restoration, and the scheme was not revised until the founding of Durham University in 1832.

Cosin's successor as bishop was Nathaniel Lord Crewe who was again

Early arms, Durham University

keen to exercise a temporal as well as a spiritual authority in the fashion of his medieval predecessors. A man much in favour with Charles II and James II, he was appointed Lord Lieutenant of the County Palatine on 4 November 1674 and entered his diocese on 9 June 1675 as much as a secular lord as a pastor, with a considerable cavalcade accompanied by running footmen. The 1687 Declaration of Indulgence cancelled the penal laws which had previously discriminated against Nonconformists and Roman Catholics, including religious tests as qualifications for any office. Crewe tried to put this policy into operation but found himself isolated and without support. At the Glorious Revolution the Dean of Durham, Denis Granville, fled the country in support of King James. Crewe vacillated and stayed, siding with William of Orange by voting for the motion of the Convention of January 1689 that James 'having withdrawn himself out the kingdom, has abdicated the Government, and that the throne is hereby vacant'.

In 1700, at the age of 67, Crewe married a second time. His bride was a young heiress aged 24, Dorothy Forster of Bamburgh in Northumberland. She predeceased him and their combined wealth provided the basis of his extensive charitable works which survive into the 20th century. He died in 1721.

It was in Crewe's episcopate that Sir John Duck moved into prominence. Duck was a humble butcher's apprentice in Durham City. The omen of a gold jacobus coin dropped at his feet by a raven inspired a career of increasing prosperity in coal-owning. In 1680 Duck was mayor of Durham and a justice of the peace. After being made a baronet in 1687 he endowed a hospital at Great Lumley. Duck died in 1691 — an archetypal member of the new gentry that was emerging in the county.

*Blagraves House,
Barnard Castle*

VII Eighteenth-Century County Durham

Durham was not a non-juring county and saw no response to the 1715 rising, despite the Jacobite sympathy of Durham City and the history of eminent non-juring personalities — George Smith of Burn Hall, non-juring 'bishop of Durham'; Denis Granville, Dean of Durham; and John Cock, vicar of St Oswald's in the city. In 1695 Celia Fiennes noted, after a fleeting visit: 'There are many papists in the town, popishly affected, and daily increase . . .' Indeed, as if to confirm this, in 1780, the year of the Gordon riots, Major Floyd remarked on the '. . . prodigious numbers of Catholics in . . . [Durham City] . . . This place . . . prodigious over-run with clergy, who in all countries take up a great deal more room than they ought, and eat out all the industrious and useful . . .'. But in 1715 no local contingent was raised and the county only provided a temporary resting-place at Whitesmocks for the body of Lord Derwentwater. In the '45 rebellion the County Militia was called out but took no part although soldiers were regularly billeted in or near Durham City. In late January 1746 on his way to Culloden to confront the Pretender, the Duke of Cumberland passed through Durham where the mayor and corporation received him ceremoniously, while the County M.P., George Bowes, presented him with a horse.

The earliest sections of the county's own regiment were formed in 1758 when the second battalion of the 23rd Foot was made into a distinct corps, named the 68th Regiment, with John Lambton as first Colonel, and in 1759 when, under the Act of 1757, the Durham Regiment of Militia was raised with the Earl of Darlington, of the Vane family, as Colonel. The Militia was intended for home defence, and was organised on a county basis with local gentry as officers and ordinary soldiers picked by ballot. (The 68th Foot, after operations on the French coast, embarked on long tours of duty in the West Indies until 1806, and were awarded their motto 'Faithful' for their action against the Carribs in 1764. The conversion in 1808 from Foot to Light Infantry saw the 68th training as skirmishers at the call of the bugle. Wellington described the battalion in the Pyrenees as 'the most gallant, the finest thing, he had ever witnessed'. The Durham Light Infantry was formed in 1881 and in 1968 the county regiment was merged into the new Light Infantry.

The Colours of the First Battalion, The Durham Light Infantry, were laid up on 12 December 1968.)

In industrial terms, the 18th century was one of increasing advance. The Church was not aloof from the progress. For example, Bishop William Talbot, Lord Crewe's eventual successor and a kinsman of the earls of Shrewsbury, came into the diocese in July 1722 and immediately set about promoting a bill in the House of Lords 'to enable . . . bishops . . . to make leases of their mines, not having been accustomably letten . . .' This would cover tin, lead, iron, coal and any other ores. The purpose of the bill was the aggrandisement of the bishop's wealth and showed a canny appreciation of the potential value of coal royalties. Previously ancient copyholders and leaseholders of bishopric or chapter land had not been subject to any claim by the lessor to the minerals lying under the surface of the leased lands. Sir John Eden, who was a county member of Parliament, supported the lessees whose wealth was threatened and fought the bill on their behalf in London, leaving it so mangled that it was abandoned. The bishop found himself heartily disliked for his attempt at sharp practice.

When Matthias Dunn was appointed Inspector of Mines for the three northern counties of England on the recommendation of a House of Lords Committee in 1849, in his report he commented upon the situation of the industry in the 18th century. He reminded his audience of the primitive nature of the wooden wagon-ways by which coal had been transported before the advent of cast-iron rails in 1767. Underground water from pits had been mainly raised, bucket by bucket, using horses at 'gins'. Although other systems had been tried, such as the late 17th-century chain pumps run by water wheels at Lumley Colliery, it was the steam engine which supplanted actual horse-power. Thomas Newcomen's steam engine was patented in 1710 and Dunn described it as 'an open-topped cylinder, the vacuum being created underneath the piston by injecting cold water into the cylinder, and realizing an effective pressure of from 4 to 5 lb per square inch on the piston'. In the first instance the pumps used were bored from solid wood and the diameter was thus not more than about ten inches. Until metal machine-castings revolutionised mining, coal which was deeper than 60 fathoms was inaccessible. So it was that the 'Grand Allies', the mining families of Ravensworth, Strathmore and Wortley, on the advice of their agents, put out such areas on long leases. They were thus left with shallow seams when the deeper Wearside seams could be exploited by better machinery.

Dunn remarks that women were employed not only in cleaning coals and barrowing them into the keels from the staiths (for which they were paid 1d to 1½d. per ton), but they were also occasionally employed underground. He also relates that a hundred years or more before his time of writing (1849), the winters were 'much longer and more severe than at present', and that for six or eight weeks at Christmas industry ceased, and plans to store coal had to be made well in advance.

The introduction of the steam engine saw the opening up of collieries at North and South Biddick, Penshaw, Rainton, Washington, Urpeth, Leefield and Pelton Fell. Whilst these collieries were developed inland, other industries continued to grow along the Tyne. Thus the glass industry, now more associated with Wearside and Sunderland, developed initially at South Shields. A Dean and Chapter lease to John Dagnia of November 1737 refers to two glass-houses on the south bank of the river Tyne. At the same time Isaac Cookson, his son John, and Thomas Jeffreys of London entered into partnership to produce crown and plate glass on the quayside at South Shields. In Sunderland by 1772 there were three green-bottle houses and one flint-glass house on the quayside.

The shipbuilding industry at Sunderland grew with the need for keels as the coal industry prospered. By the end of the 18th century there were about 20 shipbuilding yards there. John Bailey in his 1807 House of Commons report notes that 19 ships were built at Sunderland in 1790, with an average tonnage of 144 tons, of which the largest was 312, and that in 1791 six were built, average tonnage 202 tons, the largest being 356 tons.

Desire for improvements in communications and transport came with increased sophistication of industry. There was more than one proposal to build a canal into the south-west part of the coalfield, from the West Auckland area to the lower Tees. But it was the vision of a river Wear navigable from Durham to the sea which held the imagination of many throughout the century. That vision was a chimera.

In 1705 a petition and bill to make the river Wear navigable was sponsored by the Durham city guilds of Mercers, Grocers, Haberdashers, Ironmongers and Salters. The Wear Improvement Bill was passed in 1717 after an initial defeat by the Newcastle upon Tyne lobby in 1706, and despite the bishop's half-hearted attempt to protect his interests. The River Wear Commissioners were established, with, at first, objectors among the appointments — but they did not attend meetings. It was found that a vast number of rocks would need to be removed from the river between Durham and Chester-le-Street for a truly navigable route to become reality. A fine statue of Neptune was erected in Durham market-place in 1729, perhaps to symbolise the proposed union of Durham and the sea, but despite further proposals in 1754 and 1796 the vision faded as it came face to face with the reality of steam traction. In her visit to Durham in 1695 Celia Fiennes had rightly commented that

Tyne keel

St Thomas's church,
Stanhope

'The river [Wear] runs almost round the town and returns againe, that casts the citty into a tryangular; its not navigeable nor possible to be made so because its so full of rocks and vast stones, makes it difficult for any such attempt . . .'.

The agricultural pattern of the county had changed by the end of the 17th century from a great mass of smallholdings to a smaller number with a customary area of about a hundred acres which provided a greater potential for prosperity. Enclosure of arable land proceeded during the century though 'common' rights of grazing were often maintained. Bailey, in his *General View of the Agriculture of Durham*, records 26 areas mainly of pasture enclosed in the county between 1756 and 1800 either by Act of Parliament or by agreement. Enclosure awards or agreements in the 17th century had numbered at least fifty, beginning with part of Sherburn in 1634. Wolsingham was enclosed in two parcels in 1765 and 1769, and Weardale stinted moors and pasture (25,000 acres) in 1799.

In respect of the lead industry Bailey records that by 1809 there were 86 mines working in the county mainly in Weardale and Teesdale. The mines were often leased to the London Lead Company which paid rents and royalties. Thus it was that the parish of Stanhope in Weardale, the largest in the county, was also the richest. To be appointed Rector of Stanhope (and with that to a canonry of Durham Cathedral) was, financially, highly prized. The incumbent of the parish was entitled to every 10th bin of lead-ore raised from the parish lead-mines. So the income from that source in the 18th century could run to between £2,000 and £3,000 per annum. Lead production in Weardale between 1730 and 1800 grew sixfold.

Stanhope's most famous incumbent was the saintly Joseph Butler (Rector 1725-40) who held that office together with the bishopric of Bristol which was then worth only £400 per annum. Butler was elected bishop of Durham in 1750 but survived less than two years in the post. He had, however, written *Analogy of Religion* (1736), seeking 'the way of Truth', and a classic of Anglican theology. Butler, in his primary charge to his diocese in 1751, remarks that 'it is impossible for me . . . to forbear lamenting with you the general decay of religion in this nation'. His ill-health may have made him pessimistic, but he may also have been despondent to observe how the enthusiasm of the frequent visits of the evangelistic John Wesley (d. 1791) from the 1740s onwards had captured the imagination of the county. Wesley's first sermon in County Durham had been at Sunderland in 1743 and the vigour and fortitude of the Wesleyan societies grew while missionary work in the county flourished. The county took Methodism to its heart. Today, the 'Big Meeting' of the county's Methodists takes place in the county's spiritual home, Durham Cathedral.

44

9. An early view of Staindrop, a 'green village', c.1900.

10. A recent photograph of Staindrop, showing the now tree-lined central green.

11. The Norman crypt chapel in Durham Castle, dating from 1072.

12. The nave of Durham Cathedral, constructed 1093-1133.

13. Galilee chapel, Durham Cathedral, 1175.

14. Barnard Castle, overlooking the Tees, built in the 12th century by Barnard, nephew of William Rufus.

15. Brancepeth Castle, *c.*1840.

VIII A Lead-mining County

Lead was probably worked in the upper valleys of the Wear and Tees in Roman times. Records certainly show that it has been mined since the 12th century. In the first half of the last century, when Britain was the world's leading producer, Weardale and Teesdale, as part of the North Pennine orefield, were the chief centres of lead-mining in the country. Although the industry had virtually collapsed by the beginning of this century, it is still common to hear the upper valleys of the Wear and Tees referred to as 'lead dales', a term justified not only by remembered history, but in the visible legacy of mining, working and transporting the mineral.

The bishops of Durham were the major landowners of upper Weardale, where in the 12th century the mineral rights had been granted by the king to Bishop Le Puiset. The bishops alternated between leasing out mines for periods and leaving their agents to let them to local men who sold the ore to the bishop. Either way, one-ninth of the production went to the bishop as royalty. In addition to the use of lead for roofing, glazing and pipework, the same galena ore was of value for the extraction of silver used by the bishop's own mint in Durham. In Teesdale a prominent family in the extraction of lead was the Bowes family, ancestors of the present Queen Mother. Although geological knowledge must have been rudimentary, most of the major deposits were known by the 16th century. Galena fragments in streams, particularly after storms, and even lead-tolerant plants were sought as clues. It also became evident that the ore occurrences had directional bias, the result of its association with fissures or veins. Consequently, open-casting ('hushing') or primitive bell-pit working began from the point of discovery. The former consisted of building an earth dam above the ore occurrence, digging a trench along the line of the intended hush, then releasing the water to excavate an artificial valley or gorge along the line of the vein. The process would be repeated as desired. Its effectiveness is reflected in its continued use well into the last century. In several instances the end result was a hush over half a mile in length and perhaps up to 100 ft. in depth. Bell-pits were produced by working outwards from the bottom of the shallow shaft; after some yards, however, the danger of

Entrance to lead-mine, Weardale

roof-fall necessitated a new shaft, so that a sequence of pits would evolve. Adit mines, horizontal shafts or 'levels' into the hillside, were soon preferred where practical, since they were easier to work and drain. The excavated ore and spar ('bouse') was then 'dressed' or stripped of the most obvious waste material by crushing and sieving, and then burnt or smelted to produce lead ingots. Since London was the main market, transport was by teams of pack-horses across the moors along what became known as leadways or leadgates to staiths on the Tyne, or along the Tees valley to the ports of Yarm or Stockton.

The industry emerged from its medieval phase during the 18th century within a national context of business and financial evolution. It was at this time that the two companies which came to dominate lead production in the dales were formed. The London Lead Company, known as the Quaker Company, was founded in 1692 and began with leases across the watershed on Alston Moor in Cumberland before taking extensive leases in Teesdale. By the middle of the 18th century it had also acquired leases in Weardale, as well as in the adjoining Derwent valley in Northumberland, but its main activity was in Teesdale. Its northern headquarters were established at Middleton-in-Teesdale. The imprint of the company on that settlement speaks of the size of its operation. In Weardale the major exploiter was the Blackett-Beaumont Company, begun by Sir William Blackett in Allendale (Northumberland) in 1684 and later passing to the Beaumont family. Its earliest mines were leased from the Bishop of Durham — in the early 1700s Sir William Blackett was the bishop's moormaster in upper Weardale — but the company later owned some of its own mines. Although the company came to monopolise its dale to a greater degree than did the London Company in Teesdale, its headquarters were a much more modest affair at Newhouse, near Ireshopeburn. With business and capital connections, the two companies were able to introduce techniques relating to drainage, ventilation, winding and dressing which had been developed earlier in the Derbyshire and Cornwall metallic-orefields; later, knowledge was gained from the experience of the Durham coalfield. Particularly notable introductions, all towards the end of the 18th century, were 'horse-levels', by which tubs of ore were hauled by pony from adit to dressing mill on wooden, later iron, rails; water-driven crushing mills; horizontal condensing flues. The last-mentioned, consisting of a long tunnel running up the hillside from the smeltery or 'smelt mill' to a vertical chimney, not only removed poisonous fumes, but, through periodic sweeping of the chimney and washing of the flue, enabled the recovery of the considerable lead fume. A tunnel at Rookhope in the mid-19th century extended for nearly two miles over the moors.

46

The two companies built scattered cottages with associated smallholdings in the dales in order to attract miners, washers and smelters to a relatively remote area for an industry which was subject to periods of recession. Many of the workers, therefore, were in effect miner-farmers: a dual economy existed in the dales. Given the finite lifespan of a mine, cottages could be far from current workings, so that it became common for dormitories or 'lodging-shops' to be erected at the actual place of work. Here, men and boys, having brought enough food for the working week, would have one room in which to eat and sleep and to dry clothes sodden from a dripping mine, from washing ore or from exposure to severe Pennine weather unavoidable at well over 1,000 ft. above sea level. Little wonder that life expectancy for such workers up to the middle of the last century was some 15 years below the national average. They were hardly compensated by the financial return. Miners were contracted to an agreed price for each bing of ore (8 cwt) or for each fathom driven. The ore had to be dressed ready for smelting; it had to be won by the miner's own tools, gunpowder and candles, items which were of necessity obtained from the mine's agent, who was free to fix the price. There was even a charge for sharpening the tools. Payment was normally only yearly or half-yearly, and although advances were made, interest was charged on the 'subsist' or 'lent' money so that it was possible for miners to end up in debt to their employer.

Middleton House, Middleton-in-Teesdale

During the 19th century the business sense of the two major companies was balanced by an enlightened social policy. A series of charitable schemes was made financially feasible by the return of prosperity to the industry after a long period of falling prices and under-employment. At Eggleston the London Lead Company built model houses for smelters, while Middleton-in-Teesdale was practically converted from a village into a company town. A Lead Company school was opened in 1819; a bigger one was built in 1861. A prominent architect, Ignatius Bonomi, was engaged for the design of a suitable house for the chief agent, Middleton House (1823). A year later the same architect designed the Masterton House and New Town suburb, consisting of houses, with stables, for overseers, surveyors and a doctor, and a terrace for miners. (Earlier Bonomi had designed the house of the company's Weardale headquarters in Stanhope.) A Mechanics' Institute was built with company support, and reading rooms were provided. More generally, the company had begun a workmen's contributory benefit fund, given medical attention to its miners and allocated subscriptions to local chapels. In response to such humanitarian measures by a company whose directors were Quakers, the workforce was expected to be sober and hard-working. There was a prohibition on the frequenting of public houses

Drinking fountain, Middleton-in-Teesdale

Monument to Bishop Barrington

and threat of dismissal if convicted of drunkenness; minor offences incurred a fine.

The Blackett-Beaumont Company was less obviously involved, but subscribed to the several schools built or rebuilt by Bishop Barrington in Weardale in the 1820s. The bishop hoped education in the Anglican tradition would counteract the spread of Methodism in the dale. Land and money were given for another school at Irehopesburn, and all local chapels were given support.

The period of peak prosperity for the lead industry, during the middle third of the last century as urban growth of Victorian Britain demanded more lead products, saw the advent of railways to the dales. The need to export the product had already led to the construction of passable valley roads, as well as tracks across the moor. Pack-horses were not totally superseded until after mid-century. Stanhope was linked to the Stockton and Darlington line in 1862 and Middleton to the North Eastern Railway network in 1868. Although for a while low freight rates made it possible to transport lead from Cumberland for smelting in the dales, by now the Durham mines were in decline, so that a projected — and surveyed — rail extension from Middleton to Alston failed to raise the necessary capital. That the Weardale line was eventually extended as far as Wearhead in 1895 is attributable to the richness of the upper Weardale mines and to an optimism which interpreted the general collapse of the industry as a temporary, albeit severe, depression. The earliest railway to serve the industry had been the Stanhope and Tyne line, a composite of inclined planes with stationary engines and conventional locomotives, which carried lead from Stanhope to Tyne Dock at South Shields. The Weardale Iron Company built its own line in 1846 from Rookhope to connect with this line to take iron ore to Tow Law. Lead also travelled along this line (Map 6).

Overseas competition occasioned a rapid decline in the lead industry of Durham during the 1870s. Mines and smelteries closed, and there was widespread emigration to seek employment, notably in the Durham coalfield or, further afield, to lead-mines in the U.S.A. Small companies went out of business, and the major ones eventually followed suit. The Blackett-Beaumont Company relinquished its Weardale leases in 1880; the London Lead Company, relying on its Wiregill/Little Eggleshope mines, contracted considerably and finally disposed of its Teesdale leases and assets in 1903. Lead working continued for a while as the Blackett-Beaumont leases had been taken over by the Weardale Lead Company, which was formed in 1883. Of its six mines in Weardale, it was the discovery of the Boltsburn (Rookhope) vein at the turn of the century which ensured that exploitation of the mineral was just about profitable until the early 1930s (Plate 23).

County Bridge, Middleton-in-Teesdale

48

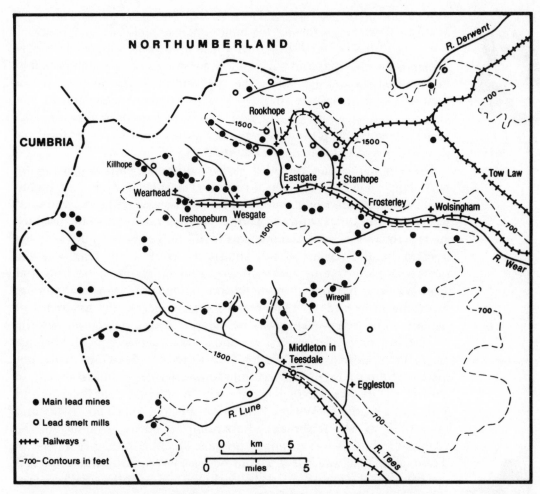

Map 6. The distribution of lead-working in Weardale and Teesdale. That part to the south of the Tees, which was added to the administrative county in 1974, is also included.

The lead industry in its later history was well served by its increasing technical efficiency, not least in the highly mechanised nature of ore concentration. This is best illustrated by the Killhope Wheel at Killhopehead. Built in 1878 by the Blackett-Beaumont Company, it made a remarkable use of water power. Its main wheel, 30 ft. in diameter, hauled tubs of ore up to the crushing mill; other wheels worked the crushing rollers and an assortment of jiggers, buddles and other separators which progressively extracted and refined the lead deposit. The water needed to provide the hydraulic power was collected by an intricate system of races above Killhope; after its use, the tail race led

Killhope Wheel

49

H. W. F. Bolckow,
ironmaster

to a second plant at Burtree Pasture, three miles away, and then on again to Westgate, a further five miles downstream.

The last phase of the lead industry also drew some support from new demands for fluorspar and barytes. The former was now sought as a flux in aluminium smelting and in the steel industry; also as a source of fluorine-based chemicals. Barytes was the source of barium for the chemical industry. Previously both minerals had been discarded as waste ('gangue'), and thus many of the tips were now reworked for these deposits. Two fluorspar mines remain today.

Other minerals had provided earlier additional employment in the lead dales. The earliest was Frosterley marble, a dark and highly fossiliferous metamorphic limestone, attractive when polished, and used as early as the 13th century in Durham Cathedral. Whinstone, used for stone setts and in road-making, was found in Teesdale, and was given a boost by the advent of rail transport. More widespread was the quarrying of limestone for fertilisers, cement and for the iron and steel industry, but the most significant activity was ironstone mining, especially in Weardale. Limonite is found alongside the fissured lead deposits. The first working was by Charles Attwood, who formed the Weardale Iron Company in 1842 and worked deposits in Middlehope Burn. These initially supplied his blast furnace at Stanhope Dene, but distance from coal soon induced him to transfer the smelting activity to Tow Law. Ore was also in demand from Consett and from Bolckow and Vaughan's works at Witton Park (near Bishop Auckland, 1848) and after 1850, at Middlesbrough. Expansion of ironstone mining in the Cleveland Hills, however, finally brought limonite mining to an end in Teesdale in 1880 and led to a contraction in Weardale, where the last operation, at Rookhope, closed in 1905. A measure of the significance of iron ore extraction may be taken from the estimate that the tonnage removed in little more than half a century was comparable to that removed over many centuries of lead mining. Certainly at its peak, the Weardale Iron Company labour force of 1,700 men was far in excess of the number ever employed by either the Blackett-Beaumont or London Lead Companies. Statistics notwithstanding, however, with the extraction of both minerals having now passed into history, it is as 'lead dales' that the area is remembered.

Blast furnace,
Stanhope Dene

John Vaughan,
ironmaster

50

IX   The Rise of Coal

Coal provides a vital strand in any history of County Durham — economically, socially and politically. The Durham coalfield has been exploited on a commercial basis longer than any other in the country, with its early seaborne exports, albeit under the tag of 'Newcastle coal', playing a key supportive role in the growth of London. In more recent times, the history of the county *is* the history of coal-mining, with the extraction, movement and utilisation of the mineral significantly determining the population and employment patterns and settlement types.

The earliest beginnings of coal exploitation are obscure, although evidence of workings on the south bank of the Tyne during the Roman period is suggested. The *Boldon Book* of 1183 refers to 'coalsmiths' at Bishopwearmouth and Sedgefield and 'colliers' at Escomb. Less than a century later there are references to profits from the prince bishop's coal-mines and workings at Gateshead and Whickham, by which time 'Newcastle coal' was already being shipped to London. Extraction in the vicinity of the Tyne and, later, Wear was facilitated by the incised river courses, which exposed the top seams to permit surface workings or shallow adits into the valley sides. The first area worked was that between the tributaries Team and Derwent, with wheelbarrow or pack-horse being used to transport the coal to wharves ('staiths') on the Tyne.

From the second half of the 16th century output expanded as wood became less plentiful and the country slowly began to turn towards a coal-burning economy. At the same time the Reformation brought a boost when the Crown took over the Church's mines, which had been worked on a restrictive basis, and leased them out. Particularly important was the 99-year so-called 'Grand Lease' of the Gateshead and Whickham mines to Newcastle merchants. The power of the Newcastle burgesses and the monopoly of the Tyne, however, were soon broken when exploitation began in the vicinity of the tidal Wear below Chester-le-Street.

A transport revolution was now under way. Horse-drawn wagons ('chaldrons'), running on wooden planks or wagon-ways, appeared in the mid-17th century. An efficient haulage system was imperative as the

Early coal wagon, the logo of Beamish Museum

51

scale of operation and distance from waterside staiths increased. Flanged and then cast-iron wheels were introduced, while at Tanfield in 1727 the barrier of a ravine was overcome by what is now acknowledged as the first railway bridge in the world.

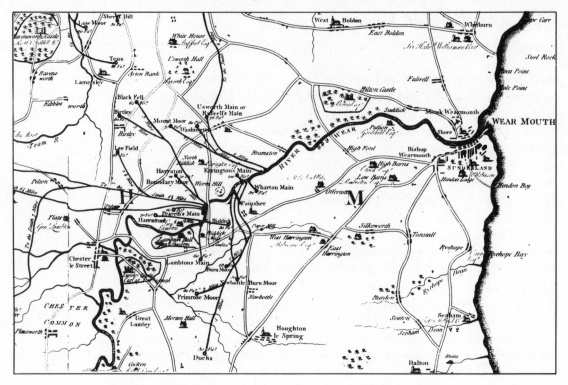

Map 7.   Coal wagon-ways on staiths on the lower Wear, 1788.

The network of horse wagon-ways just prior to the next technological advance is given in Gibson's map of 1787 (Map 7). About this time some three-dozen pits were linked to the navigable reaches of either the lower Tyne or Wear. The longest was the nine-mile line from Pontop Pike to staiths on the Tyne at Dunston, but most were under half this length since land carriage was still costly. Length and gradient were dependent on the strength of one horse. It is possible to gauge the manner of transport and scale of operation from Plate 26, where the horse, having provided the motive power on the flat, can be seen following the coal chaldron on the down incline, with hand-brake being applied by the rider, to the staith and waiting keel. Each chaldron carried 53 cwt; a keel had a capacity of 20 tons. On the Wear the flat-bottomed keels daily sailed on the ebb tide to Sunderland for transfer of cargo to sea-going colliers; the return journey upriver was by pole-work and manual haulage. On the Tyne high level staiths with coal 'drops' were introduced by the mid-18th century, thereby allowing the loading onto keels or even colliers, independent of the tide. The first coal drops on the Wear were not erected until 1812.

At the beginning of the 19th century the shipment of County Durham coal from the two rivers was approaching 2,000,000 tons. Termed 'sea-coal', its output and trade greatly overshadowed the importance of the county's 'land-sale' mines, even though the latter were scattered over the whole exposed part of the coalfield and had been worked since equally early times. The crippling cost of land transport and lack of strong market, however, restricted the scale of working, so that by 1800, for instance, many of the mines were still being operated seasonally or on demand. Over half of the workings employed fewer than 10 men; in contrast, nearly all the sea coal-mines employed over one hundred. It was the experience gained in the working and haulage of sea coal that provided a basis during the 19th century for the spread of deep mining and the growth of railways.

The change from horse-drawn to steam-powered locomotion was a staggered process. The first advance was the advent of the stationary steam haulage engine to pull wagons up inclines. This may be seen as a logical development from their initial use for vertical shaft winding. The first one was in use at Birtley, near Chester-le-Street, in 1805. There then followed the moving or travelling steam engine, as it was termed. George Stephenson, engineer to the Killingworth pit in southern Northumberland, completed his first locomotive in 1814 to haul wagons along the colliery railway of Lord Ravensworth. In 1822 he was engaged by the Hetton Colliery to construct a railway to the port of Sunderland eight miles away (Plates 27 and 28). The varied terrain, however, contained sections which were too demanding for his locomotives, so a hybrid railway emerged, with stationary engines and self-acting inclines on the steeper gradients and travelling locomotives on the level stretches.

The longest and most spectacular hybrid construction was the Stanhope and Tyne Railway, designed to carry lead, lime and coal from Weardale past the Consett area to South Shields. When completed in 1834, the route incorporated nine stationary engines, five self-acting inclines and had horse-drawn sections in addition to steam locomotives on the level stretches.

George Stephenson's most famous project, the Stockton and Darlington Railway of 1825, was also a hybrid transport system. The line began at Witton Park Colliery with haulage by two stationary winding engines, and it was only from the foot of the Brusselton incline (West Auckland) through Darlington to Stockton Quay that wagons were pulled by a steam locomotive. The story is one of the romances of industrial history,

North Road station, Darlington

53

Locomotion No. 1

with the overall vision and drive of Edward Pease and several other fellow Quakers triumphing over the lack of support and scepticism from colliery owners and Stockton merchants, even though the latter had long sought a solution for the land-locked coalfield of south-west Durham. Various wagon-ways had been considered, even a canal, in an effort to move coal to the navigable lower Tees, so that the county's third river might join in the sea coal trade to south-east England. The parliamentary bill was finally given royal assent in 1821, and on 27 September 1825 the world's first public railway was opened. Hundreds of spectators lined the route to watch the iron horse *Locomotion Number 1*, with George Stephenson and his brothers James and Ralph on the footplate, haul a train of 38 wagons of coal, merchandise and passengers. A superior passenger coach, called *The Experiment*, carried the satisfied

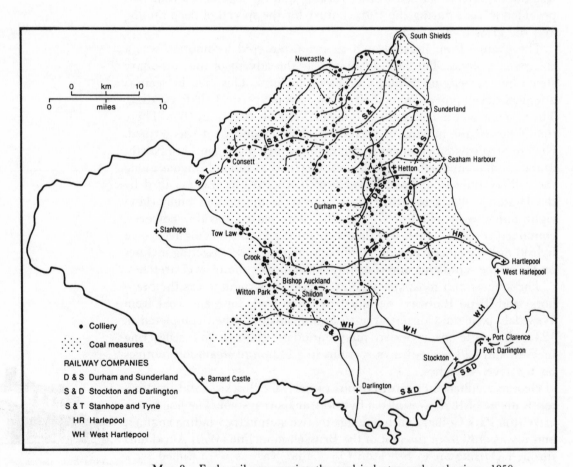

Map 8. Early railways serving the coal industry and coal mines, 1850.

54

proprietors and committee of the company. Speeds of up to 12 m.p.h. were attained on its four-hour trip to Stockton. In passing, it may be recorded that Stephenson also designed most of the bridges for the line, including the world's first iron rail bridge, over the Gaunless at West Auckland. For the crossing of the Skerne in Darlington, however, he engaged an eminent architect, Ignatius Bonomi, then road and bridge surveyor to the County. The bridge, still extant, is shown in John Dobbin's painting of the opening of the railway — Plate 29. The price of coal in Darlington dropped immediately from 18 to 12 shillings a ton, and eventually to 8s. 6d. The Stockton and Darlington Railway confirmed that the monopoly of sea coal was broken. Commercial mining now spread rapidly across the formerly land-locked parts of the county in conjunction with the growth of railways, so that these other areas also, in effect, became producers of sea coal. In less than a decade over 30 collieries were using the Stockton and Darlington Railway. Such was the congestion of vessels on the Tees that the line had already been extended downriver to Port Darlington (Middlesbrough) on the south bank. On the opposite bank Port Clarence was the new terminus for the Clarence Railway, built in 1833. Further new docks were opened along the coast at Seaham Harbour (1831), Hartlepool (1835), Sunderland (1837) and West Hartlepool (1847) as a succession of west-to-east lines brought coal for export (Map 8).

Clarence Railway Company arms

The number of outlets reflects the size of pent-up demand, although each in turn represents the strategy of particular entrepreneurs as they sought to challenge or break an existing port tax or carriage monopoly. Mineral and mineral line were thus interdependent — and both were the basis for a distinctive industrial growth as the century progressed. In the words of Timothy Eden, 'coal begat locomotion and locomotion begat more coal and more coal begat more industries'.

Coat of arms, Sunderland District

X A Mining World

Stephenson's safety lamp

Throughout the 19th century the Durham coalfield was the country's leading producer. Within the county a mining world evolved as some 500 pits were sunk and activity spread across the whole field, exploiting both the shallow seams in the west and the deeply concealed measures of the east. Several factors combined to make this activity possible. One was the spread of the rail network, as we have seen. Another was the increasing ability to excavate, drain and ventilate deeper workings, skills learned from sea coal-mines. The Newcomen engine and, later, the Watts steam engine were both applied early to extract water where flooding threatened. Ventilation was improved by the sinking of double shafts; the same free flow of air lessened the chance of the build-up of pockets of gas, while the invention of the safety lamp in 1815 further encouraged deeper exploitation. While many existing collieries were therefore rejuvenated by being able to tap deeper seams, for the first time it became technically feasible to sink shafts through the Magnesian Limestone, which conceals the eastern half of the field with a capping 800 ft. in thickness. The opening of Hetton colliery in 1822 in this section of the coalfield on the East Durham plateau therefore marked the beginning of a new era (Plate 28). Before this sinking the condition or, indeed, the existence of coal at this depth had been a matter of speculation. When in 1846 Monkwearmouth colliery was sunk to a depth of 1,700 ft. — the deepest in the country, if not the world, at the time — owners were prepared to spend four or five years on shaft sinking. Such length of operation was an indication of the increasing demand for coal — for the iron and, later, steel industry, shipbuilding and engineering, for gas lighting, for the railways themselves, which were consumers as well as transporters, and for export overseas as the traditional London market was lost to inland coalfields nearer the capital. The Durham coalfield proved uniquely able to supply a variety of coals for these different markets — coking, steam, gas, household. The deposits were exploited accordingly.

Two summary statistics of output and employment indicate the dramatic expansion. At the beginning of the 19th century the county was

56

producing no more than 2,000,000 tons; in 1913, its peak year, output reached 41,500,000 tons. Over the same period the number of miners rose from fewer than 10,000 to 165,000. The significance of the latter statistic is put into context when compared with employment in agriculture. In 1800 farming was the leading occupation, employing perhaps 10 times more people than mining; by 1913 the roles were reversed, with miners now many times more numerous than agricultural workers. The result was the creation of dozens of new colliery or pit villages, a new feature in the Durham countryside. 'The characteristic appearance of no district in the world is more strikingly marked' was how the text accompanying Hair's *Sketches of the Coal Mines in Northumberland and Durham* (1844) began. The speed of landscape change is what impressed another early reporter, a Sub-Commissioner to the Royal Commission on the Employment of Children (1841): 'Within the last ten or twelve years an entirely new population has been produced. Where formerly there was not a single hut or a shepherd, the lofty steam-engine chimneys of a colliery now send their volumes of smoke into the sky, and in the vicinity is a town called, as if by enchantment, into immediate existence'.

Both the sinking of colliery and erecting of colliery village were often a unified operation. Entrepreneurs, whether titled county gentry, Quaker businessmen or outside industrialists, often had little choice if they wished to establish at speed an industrial enterprise employing several hundred men in a rural setting. The fact that Durham was a county of relatively high agricultural wages further emphasised the need for the inducement of colliery housing. The response was remarkable. By 1913 nearly 49,000 tied colliery houses had been erected. The occupants, over 260,000, made up more than one-fifth of the total county population. Two-fifths of all miners were in 'free' tied housing, another tenth were in 'free' rented accommodation, but since this exclusive male operation was peculiarly dependent on being 'serviced' by womenfolk in a family operation, it is the proportions for married workers which give a more meaningful sociological picture. Over two-thirds of married miners enjoyed 'free' housing, and nearly another fifth were in 'free' rented accommodation. Such proportions were unique among British coalfields.

A temporary encampment of shaft sinkers and builders was the first indication that a colliery enterprise was under way. The end product was the pit and its pioneer settlement. The former, alongside the railway, consisted of a complex of shafts, engine house and winding gear, screens (to sort the coal) and perhaps coke ovens, blacksmiths' and carpenters' shops. The colliery cottages or, later, houses, were erected in straight rows, many perhaps built of brick made on site of brick-clay extracted from the colliery shaft, and with the unmade streets perhaps named after members of the owners' families or fellow directors who had subscribed to the share company. The first row was occupied by the shaft sinkers — until their work was done and the elite core moved on to the next operation. If the enterprise was of some size, then a superior row was designed for colliery officials, with a separate, detached villa for the manager.

In the early pit villages there were no facilities, so that society above ground was as raw as the life beneath could be brutal. Such pioneering conditions, the subject of novels by Harold Heslop, were memorably summarised by Sidney Webb: 'There were no Co-operative Societies; no Miners' Hall; no workmen's clubs; no schools; no religious or philanthropic institutes or missions; hardly any Friendly Societies; no insurance and no savings banks; no music, no organised recreation of any sort; nothing but (from 1830 onwards) an absolutely unrestricted number of beer-shops'. Carters or hawkers supplied the bulk of pro-visions, and continued to play an important role after the first shops had appeared. In time home-meetings were transferred to Nonconformist chapels. The established church often followed, but it was not until towards the end of the century that both a working men's club and a row of bungalows for 'aged miners' were built. The latter, funded by the recently-formed Durham Miners' Union from voluntary contributions of workmen, coal owners and individuals, were a needed adjunct, since colliery tied housing had to be vacated when employment ended — for whatever reason.

Pit villages were peopled by those drawn in locally and from neigh-bouring counties, from the lead-working dales to the west and from other mining areas such as Wales and Cornwall, besides a contingent from Ireland. In the early collieries miners were hired or bonded on a year-to-year basis, a practice similar to that used in agriculture. For a small sum of bounty money a worker was tied for the year, although this did not guarantee continuous employment. In fact, owners might close the pit for brief periods in an attempt to influence the market price of their product. Even in good times the bond gave owners the right to fine workers for a wide range of 'offences'. Together with 'tied' housing, the mine-owners thus had absolute domination. The bond was not finally abolished until 1872, following the efforts of the Durham Miners' Association, formed in 1869 and successor to three earlier short-lived unions, the earliest in 1825. A year before the bond was abolished, an annual event was instituted which became a clear expression of unity — the Durham Miners' Gala. The county town was the venue for the 'big meeting', where for one day a year the members of every colliery lodge assembled to combine carnival with rousing speeches from their leaders. Back in the villages, status and position were rigidly demarcated in the

Miners' Hall, Durham   battle to win coal.

The pit officials consisted of manager and under-manager, with over-men and their deputies to supervise operations underground. Below ground there were different categories of 'miners' based on age and experience — and strength. The most usual sequence for a lad was to pass from trapping (operating doors to regulate air ventilation and to allow tubs to pass through), putting (manoeuvring empty tubs to the face and bringing out full ones to form sets at the landing, either by hand or, as the century progressed, by pony — if headroom permitted), to hewing and filling. The hewers, the coal winners, were paid on piecework, in relation to the market price of the product and with allowance for the particular geological condition. In order to overcome inequality in working conditions, and thus in rewards, cavils or ballots were drawn for each seam every quarter. By such cavilling each team of marras (three pairs, one for each of the three shifts) was allocated a particular flat or district, with its own particular rate, for the following 13 weeks. All the time each tub was scrutinised for its stone content. If it exceeded four per cent, the whole was 'laid out', that is the company took the coal and the hewer received nothing. For the actual work the pitman was provided with an oil lamp and a shovel, but nothing else — no protective clothing, no helmet, not even his prime tool — the pick.

Davy safety lamp

The actual working conditions were confined, hot, arduous — and dangerous. Quite apart from the possible cumulative effect of coal dust and flickering oil lamp on lung and eye, serious injuries were almost commonplace, while in many pits fatalities could average one a year. It was the major accidents, however, that highlighted for the non-mining world the danger of work underground — Felling 1812 (92 killed), Newbottle 1815 (51), Haswell 1844 (95), Burradon 1860 (76), Seaham 1880 (164), Trimdon 1882 (74), Stanley 1909 (168). It was after the first of these listed disasters that a Society for the Preventing of Accidents in Coalmines was founded in Sunderland. Sir Humphry Davy was approached, and the result was the invention of the miner's safety lamp. (By coincidence, George Stephenson was producing a similar lamp simultaneously.) It is ironic to consider that the invention may not have reduced the number of deaths in mines, since owners were encouraged to exploit deeper seams or re-open others closed because of the danger of explosion.

The exploitation of coal transformed large areas of the county's landscape during the 19th century. The activity gave rise to numerous pit villages where nothing had existed before, more than doubling the number of villages in the county. It also transformed the character of many existing villages or small market towns, and was also the most important factor in the growth of the county's largest towns, such as Sunderland and Gateshead (Plate 30). In short, coal exploitation,

59

trans-shipment or utilisation was the basis for industrial growth and population concentration during the century when County Durham was in the forefront of the Industrial Revolution.

Penshaw monument

16. St Mary's church, Seaham.

17. Raby Castle.

18. Bowes Museum, designed by Jules Pellechet for John Bowes and his French wife, and built 1869-94.

19. Finchale Priory, three miles from Durham beside the river Wear, built in the 12th century.

20. Raby Castle, strongly fortified in the 14th century, and home of the powerful Neville family.

21.   Stockton High Street, *c*.1790.

22.   Church Street, West Hartlepool, *c*.1910.

23. Boltsburn lead mine, Rookhope, Weardale, *c.*1900.

24. Consett ironworks, mid-19th century.

25. Jarrow steelworks, *c.*1900.

XI The Industrial Revolution: Industries, Towns, and Personalities

Between the first national census of 1801 and the First World War the population of the county increased almost tenfold. The growth was not evenly spread. The western third of the county, consisting of Weardale and Teesdale with their intervening moorlands, did not share in the increase; neither did those market towns which were unable to attract industry during a century of unprecedented manufacturing growth. Thus centres such as Barnard Castle, Stanhope or Sedgefield, which were in the top 20 by size in 1801, slipped into insignificance in statistical terms. In contrast, other selected centres expanded and other entirely new settlements sprang into being. Apart from coal-mining settlements, there was often dependence on one industry — coal-exporting, shipbuilding, iron and steel, railway engineering. Industrial growth was often spectacular, innovative and directed by energetic Victorian captains of industry who could be both ruthless and philanthropic (Plate 31). The county provides a variety of such examples during the period when it was at the forefront of the Industrial Revolution.

Market cross, Barnard Castle

The earliest and clearest example of a single-industry company town is Seaham Harbour. Before its development, the Wear and Tyne were the only outlets for the growing export of coal. In 1819 Charles Stewart, former soldier and ambassador, later the third marquis of Londonderry, married into County Durham aristocracy. His wife, Frances Anne Vane-Tempest, was heiress to extensive property and coal-mines. Londonderry took control of his wife's estate and in 1821 bought the extensive Seaham estate, five miles south of Sunderland, determined to build his own port for the export of coal. He was stimulated by an earlier plan for the area, by knowledge that Sunderland was unable to cope with the increasing number of colliers and by a wish to bypass the river keelmen to effect a dramatic saving in transport costs. He was well served by his agent or viewer, John Buddle. Together they contacted and engaged the designer of the original dock plan (William Chapman), sought the advice of the leading civil engineers of the day (Thomas Telford, John Rennie), engaged an eminent architect (John Dobson) to design the accompanying town, and arranged loans.

St Mary's church, Barnard Castle

61

Statue of the 3rd Marquis of Londonderry, Durham

Work eventually began in 1828 and the first coal from his Rainton pit, conveyed on his own railway, left Seaham Harbour in a new collier, *Lord Seaham*, in 1831. Increasing demand necessitated enlargement of the dock in 1845 (Plate 34). Even so, continued success forced Londonderry to build and operate a railway as an overflow line to Sunderland where new docks had just opened. He died in 1854, but the momentum continued and another dock enlargement was made in 1905. By 1914 Seaham had a population of over 15,000, having been a fishing hamlet in tiny Dalden Creek at the beginning of the 19th century — a 'desert spot' according to Dobson. It is a pity that Dobson's gracious architecture remained on the drawing board, for his twin stone-faced Regency crescents flanking a central clocktower, with the railway emerging beneath to reach the harbour, would have been a fitting monument to an aristocrat who himself lived in the grand manner. But Londonderry, a determined and astute man, had insisted at the time that resources be directed to completing the harbour.

While Seaham Harbour might have been called 'Londonderry', another new town *was* frequently called after its founder during mid-century. The story of 'Jackson's Town', or West Hartlepool, begins nearby at the ancient borough of Hartlepool, which in 1801 had shrunk to under 1,000 inhabitants, with its natural harbour — the only one on the Durham coast — virtually silted up. In 1832, under the inspiration of Christopher Tennant, the Hartlepool Dock and Railway Company Act was passed. Port Darlington and Port Clarence had recently opened on the Tees, but the physical advantages of a dock in a natural harbour as opposed to a terminal in a shallow, tidal river, as well as the charging of lower port dues, brought instant success. The first coal cargo was exported in 1835; within six years its line was carrying more coal than any other and through its dock was passing one-quarter of all northeast coal shipments. In 1836 the Stockton and Hartlepool Railway Company was formed and linked the Clarence Railway to Hartlepool. A dominant figure in the new company was Ralph Ward Jackson, a Stockton solicitor with plans of his own. When the Hartlepool Company proved obstructive, Jackson soon struck out for an independent outlet, and in 1844 the short-lived agreement was dissolved and the Hartlepool West Harbour and Dock Company was formed.

Hartlepool fisherman, 18th century

The site chosen was in the same tidal basin as the old borough, one mile to the south-west, consisting of 'sand-banks, mossy swamps and agricultural fields'. In 1847 the first dock was opened and immediately became the new rail terminus, the connection to Hartlepool being severed. In the same year the settlement was acknowledged as *West* Hartlepool for the first time. A series of docks quickly followed; by 1860 they constituted overwhelmingly the most important port in north-east England, with the declared value of its merchandise that year being three times that of all the other ports combined. The West Hartlepool Company, under the direction of its chairman, Jackson, boosted coal exports through acquisition of a dozen collieries which were thus tied to the port. A large proportion of the country's timber imports was received; grain and general cargo traffic were considerable. Jackson built two massive warehouses to encourage commerce and began a steamship line to foster the amount of registered tonnage. Although the wider dream of being the fishport for Leeds and outlet for the West Riding — in short, of being 'Liverpool on the east coast' — remained unrealised, important manufacturing concerns were also attracted, especially shipbuilding, iron foundries and iron smelting.

Font at Hart (Hartlepool)

The settlement accompanying the industrial growth can also be seen as the response to Jackson's drive, both directly and indirectly. On the streets running south from the docks the leading civic buildings were on sites and built of stone given by the company, perhaps with an additional personal donation by its chairman. When, on his initiative, a Board of Improvement Commissioners was established in 1854, Jackson, as founder and leading citizen, became the obvious chairman. Within six years, however, his reign in West Hartlepool ended in ignominy.

An investigation into the Company revealed excessive borrowing, but, more significantly, the original Act had empowered the raising of capital for the railway and harbour only. The Company had therefore acted illegally in acquiring collieries and ships. Although it was acknowledged that Jackson's zeal had been for company, rather than personal, gain, resignation was inevitable. Jackson's town, however, continued to grow, with iron, steel and rolling mills linked to a major shipyard providing the industrial background. By 1914 the population of West Hartlepool, at 64,000, was more than three times that of the old borough nearby; its civic status was also superior, having been elevated to a County Borough in 1901 (Plate 22). Within the town the founder's name lived on, from Jackson Dock, Memorial Park, school and imposing statue, to a hotel and public house.

If West Hartlepool was a Victorian new town, Jarrow, of ancient foundation, became a Victorian company town, dependent on the shipyard of Charles Mark Palmer. Born in South Shields the son of a ship-owner, Palmer was subsequently knighted for his contribution to industrial and civic life. He was Jarrow's first mayor, following his successful campaign to achieve borough status in 1875, and was M.P. in the 1890s and at the turn of the century. He was chairman of his shipbuilding company until retirement in 1893, having begun the venture jointly with his brother in 1851.

Coat of arms, Hartlepool M.B.

63

The Jarrow Yard became renowned for its rapid rise, vertical integration and innovative product. Palmer recognised that the future of navigation lay with iron vessels powered by steam, and in 1852 his yard launched the first iron, screw-driven collier, the *John Bowes* (Plate 35). His confidence and conviction were reflected in the scale of the celebrations for the 300 guests invited to the birth of the world's first tramp steamer. What Stephenson had demonstrated with rail transport a quarter of a century earlier, Palmer was about to demonstrate on the sea. The *John Bowes* was of special significance to the North-East, for it signalled the region's reply to the advantage which railways were bestowing on Midland coalfields in supplying the London market. The new steam collier cut the time of the round trip to London to five days, compared with the traditional sailing vessel which required a month or more, depending on weather conditions. The new vessel was not only faster; it was bigger and took water as ballast rather than earth and stone. The former, naturally, was more easily and cheaply loaded and disposed of.

In 1854, under the stimulus of the Crimean War, the yard constructed the first iron-clad battleship, *The Terror*, which had rolled armour plates. A wide variety of naval vessels was subsequently built. In 1872 Britain's first oil-tanker, the *Vaterland*, left the slipway. By now the yard was a complete shipbuilding factory in a mighty, integrated industrial enterprise. Coke came from the company's collieries in north-west Durham. Ore from the company's mines in Cleveland and Spain was conveyed in its own steamers to the wharf at Jarrow, where blast-furnaces, steelworks and rolling mills produced plates and bars. A series of workshops, from engine- to cabinet-makers, completed the finished article. Thus, ore was taken in at one end of the yard and the finished ship came out at the other; locals joked that they built ships by the mile and cut them to required lengths.

Over 10,000 were employed at the height of the yard's operation around the turn of the century. By 1914 'Palmer's Town' had a population of over 33,000, a tenfold increase since the shipyard opened. A hospital had been built in 1870, initially for the use of shipyard employees, maintained by a company subsidy and contributions from the workforce. Earlier a building society had been started in the yard to enable skilled craftsmen to buy their own houses; a large proportion responded. Such facilities help to explain how a working-class electorate could reject a local Labour Party candidate in 1892 and elect a captain of industry for their M.P. In the two subsequent elections Sir Charles Mark Palmer was returned unopposed.

The most spectacular industrial and urban growth in absolute terms in the last century was at the mouth of the Wear. In 1801 there were three separate settlements in the area — Monkwearmouth on the north bank and Bishopwearmouth on the south, with their names revealing ancient origins, and Sunderland, on the south bank on land 'sundered', or separated, from the monastery. Their combined populations totalled 24,000; by 1914 the total of a unified County Borough had grown to over 150,000. The twin activities of coal exporting and shipbuilding were the basis of this expansion.

For over two centuries Sunderland, at the mouth of the Wear, had been a trans-shipment point between river keels and sea-going colliers. In 1800 some one thousand keelmen and boys were plying the river, between wagon-way terminals and waiting sea vessels, but as the 19th century progressed, continued success of the coal trade at Sunderland, as with its competitors, depended on the attraction of railways and the creation of port facilities.

Early railways were the Newbottle, or Lambton (1815), and Hetton (1822) lines which terminated at adjacent staiths, followed by the Durham and Sunderland (1836) westwards into the middle part of the coalfield, and Brandling Junction (1839) northwards. Its potential as a coalport, however, was handicapped by the crowded nature of the river and by navigational difficulties made worse over the years by the dumping of ballast. Formation of a Sunderland Dock and Railway Company in 1833 brought early promise, but rivalries between the north and south bank ended with a North Dock (1837) which proved too small with difficult access. A bolder plan was required if Sunderland was to compete with successful schemes elsewhere. The solution was to invite George Hudson, the 'Railway King' from York with known parliamentary ambitions, to stand as M.P. on the understanding that he would press for the necessary Acts. Hudson immediately rescued the Durham and Sunderland line from bankruptcy and pioneered a new large dock (Hudson Dock, 1850), which was excavated to the south of the river mouth. When its own southern outlet was opened, shipping was able to avoid the hazardous river mouth bar. Arrival of the Londonderry line from Seaham Harbour confirmed the need for the docks. Meanwhile collieries opening in the vicinity of Sunderland further boosted exports, which reached a peak of over 5,000,000 tons early in the present century.

The coal trade on the river encouraged the evolution of a shipbuilding industry, from river keels to sea-going wooden sailing craft to iron and, later, steel steamships. Although Sunderland came to be known as the largest shipbuilding town in the world, it did not innovate and, unlike the previously described examples, was not characterised by the dominance or drive of one particular entrepreneur. The first steam tugboat, for instance, had been built on the Wear in 1825, but it was not until the 1850s that sail began to give way to steam in the number of vessels

The 3rd Marquis of Londonderry

65

Gibside Hall

launched. Similarly, while the first iron ship left the slipway in 1852, it was only in the late 1860s that the iron shipping tonnage exceeded that of wood. The reason is related to the small-scale structure of the industry: there was a tradition of family firms, small groups of self-employed shipwrights engaged in a craft industry. Many at the same time were also timber merchants; on the other hand few had the different skills, or the capital required, for a metal-based industry. As a result, there was a proliferation of shipyards during the first half of the century, many building on a speculative basis. In 1800 the yards numbered two dozen; in the peak year of 1840 this figure had trebled and a record number of 263 vessels was launched, with a grand tonnage of 66,700. 'Every place where they can build a ship, almost, is a yard', is how Lower Wearside was described in a Royal Commission report (Plate 33). Among the many yards were the bulk of the family concerns which were to survive the wide fluctuations in demand, and change in scale and technology to become well-known names in the world of shipbuilding — Laings, Austin, Bartram, Pickersgill, Doxford. Following half a century of scale increase and amalgamations, as many as 13 firms were still operating in 1914. At that time, shipbuilding and its marine-related industries were employing some 20,000, over two-fifths of the male workforce of Sunderland, and launching around 300,000 tons of new shipping in peak years.

Early centres of the iron industry evolved towards the western edge of the coalfield, where there were shallow deposits of coking coal, also local or easily accessible supplies of ore from the Dales in the railway age. Of centres such as Tow Law, Witton Park and Consett, it is the last-named which deserves to rank among the county's list of Victorian success stories. Before the establishment of the Derwent Iron Company in 1846, the area of high moorland supported two small farms; by 1914 there was a town of 11,000. In industrial terms, the works grew within five years to be the largest iron-producer in England; the reputation for its quality of product was enhanced by its exhibits at the 1851 Great Exhibition. When after 1852 it turned to steel production, the company became the country's leading producer of steel plates for the shipbuilding industry (Plate 24).

Three of the four founding partners at Consett were Quakers. Their work ethic was reflected in the efficiency of their vertically-integrated organisation, with its own collieries, ore mines and limestone quarries. The last-named were in Stanhope and took advantage of the Stanhope and Tyne Railway. In the 1850s a branch line was built via the Stockton and Darlington Railway to give access to new ore mines at Upleatham. Both line and mines were other Quaker enterprises. Quaker philanthropy was seen in the early provision of 1,300 cottages, also the provision of elementary education, reading rooms, a company surgeon — and policemen! Their influence remained, even though in 1864 there was new management and a new name, the Consett Iron Company. By 1914 the number of tied cottages exceeded 2,700. The workforce by now was over 6,000, while the works themselves included seven blast-furnaces and over 1,000 coke ovens. It also incorporated one particularly tall chimney which pinpointed the location of Consett for miles around. Already highly visible on the edge of Durham's high moorland, this landmark symbolised the remarkable ascendancy of industry in the county during the preceding century. That ascendancy, however, and the series of notable enterprises to which it gave rise, was soon to be rudely shaken.

Ryehope pumping station

XII The County in Depression

The end of hostilities in 1918 brought hopes of the promised 'brave new world' for the county and for its working class. Overseas, the country's aggressor, the county's main pre-war economic competitor, had been forced into economic submission. At home, prosperity began to return to the county's key activities, not only coal-mining, but to shipbuilding, iron and steel, and engineering. Moreover, following wartime state control of coal-mines, there were indications that the government might look favourably on nationalisation of the industry and on other union demands. When in the county council elections of 1919 Durham became the first authority to elect a Labour majority, it seemed that the age of the working man had dawned. Certainly the working class had produced a leader of stature, appropriately from the mining industry. Peter Lee, who was working underground at the age of 10, and educated by night-class, had been chairman of Wheatley Hill parish council and Easington rural district before accepting county chairmanship. He was also general secretary of the Durham Miners' Association and was later to become president of the Miners' Federation of Great Britain (Plate 42a). Unfortunately the grand vision was not to be, as it vanished in the face of forces emanating beyond the county's boundaries. Unions had to concede defeat as the vulnerability of Durham's economy was cruelly exposed. The repercussions have become part of our social history.

The county's economic prosperity throughout the 19th century had been increasingly built on a wasting resource, coal, and on a narrow range of heavy, capital goods. All were dependent on the export market, and all had received stimulus in the years leading up to the First World War. Durham, highly vulnerable to national and international vagaries, was therefore greatly disadvantaged by the depression into which the industrialised world sank in the 1920s. Overseas countries exploited their own energy sources and manufactured their own products. Naval vessels were no longer needed and there was a surfeit of merchant vessels given the slump in world trade. Consumer industries for the home market became the basis of prosperity, for which other areas were better located. The effects of the inter-war depression were therefore severely felt in the county as its major industries went into sharp decline or showed disastrously wide fluctuations. Unemployment was well above the national level: on average over a quarter of the workforce was idle from the 1926 General Strike onwards; in the worst year of the slump in 1932 the county unemployment level reached 40 per cent; locally it was much higher.

The fortune of coal was critical, as the basis of industry and major employer. The early promise of a post-war recovery brought a peak employment figure of 170,000 in 1923. Since the most easily-exploited seams had been exhausted, extra manpower was needed to satisfy the demand for coal shipments, but then the market collapsed and, with it, the numbers employed. By 1933 they had dropped to 101,000 and, with increasing mechanisation, had only recovered slightly by 1939, a decline of one-third overall. Even these figures conceal the amount of under-employment; also that average earnings — the lowest of all coalfields — were barely above subsistence level. Further, the level of earnings was reduced for many years by the repayment of emergency relief granted during the 1926 strike, besides any debts run up with the local co-operative society. Durham miners had been ill-prepared for the six-month strike in the industry which followed the brief 1926 General Strike, for they had barely recovered from the 30-week stoppage in 1921 during which, it being deemed a trade dispute, the men had not been eligible for relief, and following which they had had to settle for lower wages and longer hours. During the desperate conditions of 1926, with the financial resources of the Durham Miners' Association exhausted, Poor Law Unions gave relief to almost a quarter of the county's population; the county education authority gave meals to school children in over 300 centres; for adults there were soup kitchens run by voluntary labour, with the aid of gifts and parcels 'on tick'.

During the 1920s a series of alleviatory schemes was inaugurated. There was London's Lord Mayor's Fund for the distressed mining areas of Durham, Northumberland and South Wales, while other organised groups, from villages to counties, 'adopted' particular Durham mining villages to target money and clothing to help relieve poverty and distress. The Miners' Federation of Great Britain organised a National Distress Fund to provide food and clothing parcels. Then there was Ministry of Labour help with lodgings and removal expenses to unemployed miners who could find work in other parts of the country; in like manner, Juvenile Unemployment Centres were set up throughout the county to transfer 'employable' boys. The Durham Labour Exchange and Durham Miners' Association even arranged to train unemployed miners for farmwork abroad. A measure to alleviate boredom and restore some human dignity was the setting up of centres by the Council of Social Service to teach unemployed miners a variety of subjects, from cobbling to country dancing and art. The 'settlements' were run by voluntary social workers; those at Spennymoor and Seaham were particularly notable. There were also projects to level some slagheaps. A more common activity on slagheaps, however, was the gathering of waste coal. This epitomised the continuing poverty which, in some villages, stemmed from an unemployment figure of 90 or 100 per cent.

Unemployment and poverty were felt no less among other industries, especially shipbuilding and repair. The graph of output showed wild fluctuations, with boom years and bad years; 1919, 1924 and 1929, for instance, were good years, but increasing foreign competition and the stagnation of international trading meant that the troughs became disastrously low. Activity remained extremely slack throughout the first half of the 1930s. In 1932 the tonnage launched was a mere five per cent of that in 1919. Casualties in economic and human terms were inevitable, the common experience being emphasised by the concentrated nature of shipbuilding communities. Workers lived near to the yards because of the 'market system' in recruiting for a fluctuating industry. The market was the pool from which the foreman drew skilled workers, who in turn selected from the market for their unskilled helpers. Workers therefore needed to be at hand for selection. In the early 1930s unemployment in both Hartlepool and Sunderland exceeded 40 per cent, but even this figure pales into insignificance compared with the experience of Jarrow.

The shipyard at Jarrow was among the six largest British shipbuilding firms, with its efficient, modern yards occupying, in the words of the President of the Board of Trade, 'one of the best sites in the world'. In 1931, however, only a single ship was launched; the next year saw the last ship completed, and when a hoped-for Admiralty order did not arrive, the yard closed, bankrupt. In 1934 all hope of any recovery was lost when it was bought by the National Shipbuilders' Security, for the consortium's aim was to 'take out' excessive capacity in the industry in the name of rationalisation. Any yard purchased had a moratorium against further shipbuilding for 40 years. In one of the poignant coincidences of history, in the same month in which the yard closed, a collier, the *Villa Selgas*, sank off the Spanish coast. Renamed several times during its long working life, the vessel had been launched at Jarrow in 1852 with great ceremony and in the presence of Palmer himself: it was the *John Bowes*.

The shipyard, although sound technically, was financially vulnerable. With hindsight, recent share policy and the purchasing of subsidiary companies was imprudent, while the overhead charges of a steelworks, idle throughout much of the 1920s, was an additional burden (Plate 25). It remains a matter of speculation whether history would have been different had any of the company's directors been on the

Villa Selgas

70

N.S.S. board. That Jarrow was up against national forces was further emphasised when an American firm wished to purchase its steelworks to establish an integrated unit. A consultant's report showed that the site would produce steel at considerable cost advantage; the response of the British Iron and Steel Federation was to demand that a fine be levied on every ton equivalent to that advantage. Not unnaturally, the scheme was dropped. The government claimed it could 'do nothing' in the situation, and that 'Jarrow must work out its own salvation'. Little wonder that the town's M.P., Ellen Wilkinson, should entitle her history of Jarrow, *The Town that was Murdered* (Plate 42b).

In 1933 Jarrow's unemployment figure reached 77.9 per cent and official estimates were that 23,000 from a town population of 35,000 were on relief. It was out of these ashes that the Jarrow 'Crusade' was born. Officially organised from the Town Hall, 200 men were selected from hundreds of applicants after vetting from the borough medical officer for a 300-mile march to London. On 5 October 1935, following a blessing by the Bishop of Jarrow, the column set off with Ellen Wilkinson at the head, accompanied for the first stage by the mayor and mayoress. Marching in step to the music of their mouth-organs by day and holding public meetings by night, they carried a 12,000-signature petition to be presented at the opening of Parliament (Plate 43).

Although the Jarrow March has gone down in the annals of the nation's social history, the 'great folk movement', as Ellen Wilkinson called it, in fact achieved little in material terms. There were even those who had been against such a demonstration. Thus, while the organisers saw it as a non-political crusade, the Bishop of Durham warned against 'revolutionary mob pressure'. He had earlier considered the miners' strike 'immoral' and warned against charity 'rotting the character'. It was the impetus of rearmament in the late 1930s which eventually brought some industrial life back to Jarrow, not least in the re-opening of the steelworks in association with Consett Iron Company.

The years of the depression were spent by many in town and village among the worst housing conditions in the country. This was officially confirmed in a national survey of overcrowding in 1936, when Sunderland (with 20 per cent of its working-class families in overcrowded conditions), Gateshead, South Shields and West Hartlepool were listed as four of the five most overcrowded county boroughs in England and Wales. The position was reiterated in the 1951 national census, when six of the nine most crowded urban districts were in County Durham. Following the First World War, conditions had been exacerbated by the initial impoverishment of local authorities, together with delay in any improvements in the housing stock of coal-owners for fear of nationalisation. The extensive 'free' colliery housing or 'rent allowance',

Coat of arms, South Shields C.B.

71

it has been argued, perpetuated some of the worst evils. On the one hand, tied housing reduced the local authorities' sense of responsibility; on the other hand, there were instances where coal-owners threatened close their mine if forced by the local authority to make particular improvements. Meanwhile, with alternative housing scarce and council rents high, families in their 'free' housing were tempted to remain, despite the frequent link between overcrowding and insanitary conditions.

Life in the inter-war environment of County Durham has been well captured in the writings of Sid Chaplin, born of mining stock in Shildon. Complementary, professional assessment of the settlements created by the industrial revolution was made by another native of West Durham, Thomas Sharp, who became a leading planner of his era (Plate 42c). He summarised the striking contrast within the county in terms of 'hills and hells' and 'beauty, beastliness and dereliction'. He brought at once an expert and insider's eye to landscapes, to which Priestley on his *English Journey* of 1933 was to bring a comparative vision. Priestley saw a similar contrast, warning any traveller against alighting at Durham railway station allured by the attraction of the city or by the thought of Weardale, for the extensive coalfield area was 'so unlovely, so completely removed from natural beauty or anything of grace and dignity contrived by man'. The centres of manufacture were no better. The whole of Tyneside was 'ruthlessly ugly . . . the very scragends of human life', with Gateshead appearing as if 'planned by an enemy of the human race' and Jarrow 'far worse' than anything he had imagined in his own fictitious, derelict shipping town of Slakeby. Here and in nearby Hebburn he was struck by the hundreds of skilled but unemployed men standing around, wearing 'drawn masks of prisoners of war . . . waiting for Doomsday'. In summary, he reflected that mining and manufacturing in Durham 'had done very well in its time for somebody, but not, somehow, for itself'.

Priestley's journey did not include Billingham, which was one of the few inter-war success stories. Here a wartime German blockade had induced government intervention to ensure production of synthetic ammonia for the manufacture of explosives; after the war the plant provided a key unit in the formation of the I.C.I. company. A fertiliser empire was built up, and in 1935 the hydrogenation of coal marked the first step in the subsequent expansion of a petrochemical industry.

Another portent of change was the 'Special Areas Act' of 1934, which marked the beginnings of political concern of central government in regional development. The whole of the county with the exception of Darlington was covered by the legislation and thus was eligible for resources to set up new estates with serviced factory premises in order

72

to attract new industry. As a result 'trading estates' were established in Pallion (Sunderland), St Helen Auckland and Team Valley (Gateshead). Attention was especially focused on the Team Valley, since it was the country's first estate (Plate 45). Set up in 1936, on its 700 acres there began to arise 'Today's Industrial City of Tomorrow', with an eminent architect, William Holford, engaged to ensure careful design. Not only was the architecture attractive and the industry 'light', but the labour force — a modest 3,000 on the three estates by 1939 — was also distinctive in that over half were females. To this extent the amelioration of male unemployment was tempered.

The general revival in the economy towards the end of the 1930s was too modest and too late to undo the effects of nearly two decades of industrial change and depression. Perhaps the best concluding summary of the overall fortune of the inter-war years is in the county's population figures. While the country as a whole increased by over nine per cent up to 1939, County Durham declined by three per cent. This first reversal since the county had helped to launch the nation's industrial revolution reflects a massive outward migration; had this movement not occurred, the tragic levels of unemployment in the county would have been even higher.

Team Valley logo

XIII   A New County

*County Durham
arms, pre-1974*

In the period now more appropriately called the second half of the
20th century than the post-war years, County Durham has undergone
significant changes — economically and socially, in terms of landscape,
even with regard to its administrative area. In many ways, therefore, it
is appropriate to speak of a new county.

The most clear-cut change was that of local government when in 1974
the county lost its northern and southern portions to the newly-created
counties of Tyne and Wear and Cleveland, respectively, but gained
Startforth Rural District from the North Riding. The latter led to the
addition of the white rose of Yorkshire to the county's coat of arms. The
adjustments left County Durham somewhat smaller in area, with its
coastline reduced to a mere 11 miles, and a population more than
halved. Our focus, however, will continue to be on the ancient geographical county between Tyne and Tees. Here the major features existing in
1945 had all been set during the inter-war years, although the wartime
economy had cut the county's unemployment rate by over two-thirds
from its 1939 figure of 15 per cent. Its staple industries were destined to
decline, even though for the second time in this century the resumption
of peacetime initially brought hopes of a new beginning.

The county's leading industry, coal, was finally taken into public
ownership in 1947. At this time it still gave employment to 108,000 in
127 pits (Map 9). Nationalisation, however, came too late in the history
of what had earlier been England's premier field. Exhaustion or flooding
of seams in the west and some thinning of seams eastwards contributed
to the fact that, despite increasing mechanisation, cost of extraction was
now well above the national average. A drop in demand, especially for
export, exacerbated by increasing oil competition in the 1960s, meant
that the Coal Board's *Plan* and *Revised Plan* for the industry proved to
be unduly optimistic. The locating of a nuclear power station on the
north bank of the Tees at Seal Sands was a further indignity, and
indicated the challenge facing the Durham coalfield. In consequence,
national ownership has had to oversee a massive contraction of the
industry as it retreated ever eastwards towards the coast. The rundown
was particularly rapid in the 1960s when half the workforce and over

*County Durham
arms, post-1974*

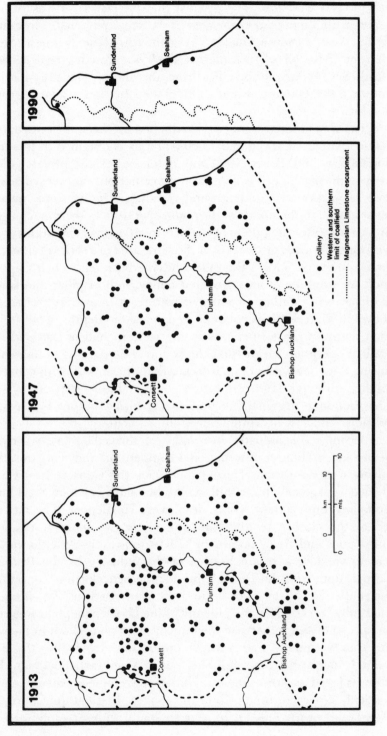

Map 9. The distribution of collieries in 1913, 1947 and 1990.

half the pits were lost. The result is that the last decade of this century begins with a mere 8,000 engaged in six remaining pits — from north to south, Westoe (South Shields), Wearmouth, Vane Tempest (Seaham), Dawdon, Murton and Easington. Each is extracting coal beneath the North Sea as far as six miles from the shore. The fully-mechanised output, 8,000,000 tons, is but a fifth of the 1913 figure, a large proportion of which was hand-hewn.

A feature of more recent coal production has been the growth of opencast working. An additional 1,000,000 tons is obtained in this manner, operated by both British Coal and, to a lesser extent, privately. Modern excavating machinery is able to uncover not only unworked seams but coal left in previous underground workings. One can only guess what passes through the minds of the crane operators as their machines scoop up in a few bites the pillars of coal left by previous generations of hewers who toiled for days or weeks over the same area in a series of subterranean embayments or 'stalls', the pillars having been left to help support the roof. An example of an uncovered honeycomb of pillar and stall mine working, representing an unusual feature of industrial archaeology, is shown in Plate 47. It is common to opencast to depths of 500 ft., deeper than many of the former pits in the western half of the field. Such a scale of operation means that the countryside is ravaged more severely during these few years of its working than it ever was with conventional mining, although land restoration is a mandatory part of any scheme. The economic argument is that the opencast output is necessary to subsidise the cost of winning deep-mined coal.

A second staple industry, iron and steel, thrived for nearly two decades before succumbing to international competition and reorganisation following nationalisation. During the 1950s the Consett Iron Company erected a large new plate mill, while the South Durham Steel and Iron Company built a new works near West Hartlepool. The latter plant led to the closure by the company of its two older works in West Hartlepool and Stockton. In the 1970s, however, even the new plant had to yield to a rationalisation of the industry by the British Steel Corporation, with the Teesside production henceforth to concentrate on the south side of the river around the giant Redcar blast-furnace and Lackenby works. Only the pipemill of the Hartlepool plant was retained for special orders; otherwise the industry was phased out in the south of the county, quietly and without opposition. Ironically, the national union leader at the time, Bill Sirs, was a West Hartlepool man. He had been replaced and the economic climate had changed when steelworking suddenly ceased in the north of the county. In 1980 the Consett works closed, and nearly 4,000 men were suddenly without a job in an area of

26. Loaded chaldron on wagon-way incline to riverside coal staith and keel, late 18th century.

27. The first coal staiths ('Lambton Drops') at Sunderland, 1815.

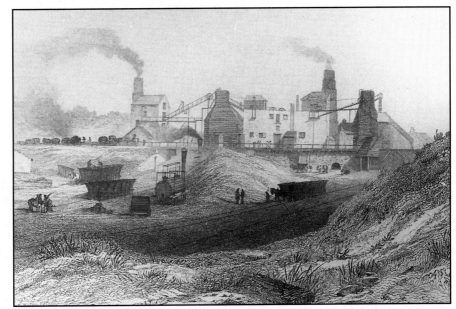

28. Hetton Colliery, the first pit to be sunk through the Magnesian Limestone of the East Durham Plateau, was opened in 1822.

29. The opening of the Stockton and Darlington Railway, 1825, painted by John Dobbin.

30. Gateshead from across the Tyne Bridge, *c.*1830.

31. Prominent Victorians in County Durham:

(a) Edward Pease.

(b) Charles Stewart, third Marquis of Londonderry.

(c) Ralph Ward Jackson.

(d) Sir Charles Mark Palmer.

32. Aerial view of the city of Durham.

high unemployment. An action campaign was formed and comparison made with the 1930s, but, unlike the 1930s, generous redundancy payments were made and capital grants or funds made available for new activities from the B.S.C., the councils, English Estates and the European Regional Development Fund. As a result, within a decade the number of job losses had been made good, although with a preponderance of female employment, and all visible evidence of the former works removed in what was described as Europe's largest reclamation scheme.

Another traditional industry, shipbuilding, which had been fully stretched during the war years, enjoyed similar early post-war prosperity. At first there was demand to replace wartime losses and reconversion of commandeered vessels, followed by a demand for cargo and bulk carriers which was given a boost by the Suez Crisis of 1956. North Sea oil brought limited activity later, but the growth of world shipping capacity, as a result of expansion in the Far East as much as in Europe, brought a succession of amalgamations so that by the end of the 1960s all the major yards were in a consortium. Continued over-capacity, with no naval business to complement its merchant vessel activity, subsequently brought the closure of yards on all three estuaries. The fate of the last shipbuilders struck echoes of Jarrow two generations earlier when the former Austin and Pickersgill yard — already an amalgam of famous Wearside yards — closed in 1989. The industry had been nationalised in 1977, and as part of North-East Shipbuilders the yard was acknowledged as the most modern commercial shipbuilding unit in the country. In fact 'yard' was an inadequate description for the massive, totally enclosed cathedral of industry. However, when controversy surrounded its last order and the government was unconvinced by possible future orders or offers to buy the yard, 2,500 men were made redundant, the last of a proud line in a town which was once the world's leading shipbuilding centre. There remains now the repair of vessels on Wearside and on the south bank of the Tyne.

Another heavy industry with particular roots in the county which has ceased in recent years is that of railway engineering. The former North East, then L.N.E.R., locomotive plant at Darlington closed in 1966. Wagon-building at Shildon survived long enough to host the 175th anniversary celebrations of the birth of the railways, including a cavalcade of steam headed by a replica of *Locomotion Number 1*, before the works finally closed in 1984.

Although the decline, or certainly the speed of decline, of the county's staple industries was not predictable in the immediate post-war years, the physical environment to which they had given rise had long been the focus of concern. With planning no longer permissive but mandatory

Coat of arms,
Darlington District

77

following the 1947 Town and Country Planning Act, the county authority was clearly faced with a formidable problem. In its 1951 *Development Plan* the prime task was boldly stated: 'to adjust the whole fabric of the settlement pattern to the likely future changes in employment'. This was no mean task since it involved some 350 settlements, half of which were mining villages established in the 19th century, the overall effect of which was to produce an unplanned and unco-ordinated pattern or, in the words of the county planning officer, 'thousands of bits of Manchester stuck in the hills'. The chosen alternative to maintaining this outdated pattern was selective investment to regroup population, thereby creating centres that could be more attractive physically, economically and socially. Settlements were therefore classified according to their predicted — or proposed — population change based on employment prospects, physical condition of property and services and on siting. Four categories of population and, therefore, investment fortune were proposed.

Although the principle of selective investment, with its implication of losers as well as winners, was accepted at county level, the fourth category caused controversy at the local level. No fewer than a third of the villages were classified 'Category D'; in these, considerable population loss was expected, no new residences were to be permitted and any investment was to be limited to the life of existing property (Plate 44). At one point an action committee was formed in south-west Durham and caused some embarrassing moments for the county authority, but the policy prevailed. It had been reaffirmed in the 1964 *Review of the Development Plan*, although the alphabetical categories were replaced by descriptive labels. During the 1960s the principle of selectivity was consistent with the prevailing concept of 'growth points'. The concept was a central feature, for instance, of the *Hailsham Report* of 1963, and lay behind the futuristic suggestion of the Northern Architectural Association of a north-south linear city through the centre of the county. Again, Washington New Town was designated (1964) to focus the growth potential of north-east Durham and south Tyneside. The county's two earlier New Towns, Newton Aycliffe (1947) and Peterlee (1947) had also conformed to the policy of regrouping population from dispersed and outworn settlements.

The catalyst for the proposed growth of Newton Aycliffe New Town was the large industrial estate, a former government Ordnance factory erected in 1940 to supply munitions during the Second World War. It lay adjacent to the Great North Road and railway, on agricultural land of indifferent quality and with no coal measures beneath. Its function of resettling population from the declining south-west coalfield brought opposition from the local authorities concerned, so that the target population was set at a modest 10,000. However, the government-appointed Corporation in charge of development argued that such a small size would inhibit the provision of facilities and eventually this target figure was twice revised. The current population is some 25,000 in a town largely constructed on garden city lines. Although Peterlee New Town has grown to a similar size over the same period under the guidance for much of the time of the same Development Corporation, its history has been distinctive, often colourful and associated with particular personalities.

The origin of Peterlee belongs to C. W. Clarke, engineer and surveyor to Easington Rural District Council. A visionary and idealist, as well as a practical engineer, it was he who had the idea of centralised development for the scatter of mining settlements on the East Durham Plateau. He persuaded his councillors to accept the idea, located a site following his survey and suggested it be named after the miners' leader who had begun his political career within the District. Clarke's findings and proposals were summarised in 1946 in an evocatively-titled volume, *Farewell Squalor*. He then attracted the attention, and ultimate support, of the Minister of Town and Country Planning for a government-appointed New Town corporation to achieve the vision. The story did not arrive at a romantic conclusion when Clarke was overlooked as the Corporation's chief architect and planner in favour of a Russian emigré, Berthold Lubetkin. Clarke subsequently became a clergyman in the Anglican church. Lubetkin, a modern architect of international repute, rejected the garden city theme as inappropriate to achieve the Minister's request for 'a miners' capital of the world', and proposed an ambitious high-rise scheme. This vision was thwarted, however, by the National Coal Board which would not agree to the necessary sterilisation of coal seams beneath the site in order to support his surface constructions. After protracted, unsuccessful discussions with the Coal Board, Lubetkin resigned frustrated and a more conventional design was adopted. However, flair returned in 1955 when Victor Pasmore, an internationally-known painter, joined the architectural team. As a result, in part of the town innovative 'cubist' housing and a rolling topography were combined to create a 'new aesthetic'. Acknowledged as 'an experiment', to many it was art rather than architecture, not least to the inhabitants who suffered from a questionable design of flat roofs on a coastal plateau 500 ft. up, from poor materials and faulty construction. For the town as a whole, the contraction of mining has meant that Peterlee has become less of a miners' capital and more of an industrial centre, facilitated by the A19 trunk route and a Corporation advertising it as 'the place to be'.

The Forum, Billingham

Billingham, already a new town in terms of buildings, having grown with the inter-war expansion of the chemical industry, approached the County Council in 1947 to seek government New Town designation. It was eventually decided that continued local authority direction would achieve quicker results. Its economic base was certainly buoyant, if specialised, with the chemical complex expanding particularly as a result of the growth of oil-based products. The population has doubled to over 40,000. In urban terms, apart from the giant apparatus of the Works and an early, central leisure complex (The Forum) opened in 1967, the townscape is conventional and unexciting. The same cannot be said for the growth centre in the north of the county.

Washington New Town was designated in 1964, in the second round of designations, following its recommendation by the County Council and support by the *Hailsham Report*. Its area already possessed mining settlements, the biggest of which was Washington, and a chemical works. It was also strategically located within the Tyne and Wear urban region to take advantage of the planned road network. Indeed, as its *Master Plan* announced, Washington was to be designed 'to cater for full motorisation'. It was accordingly laid out on a grid pattern of dual carriageways, with intersections of secondary roads every mile leading to 18 distinct settlements quaintly named 'villages' although referred to by number on the highways (Plate 46). Each settlement is given a distinctive identity through a particular architectural style and is linked to others by a complementary system of footpaths. The central feature is what would be referred to anywhere else as an out-of-town shopping centre. Although over-optimistic in its car-owning prediction — 'By the year 1976 it is expected that nearly every family will have at least one car' — its location and environmental standards have ensured success as a focus of industry and services within the broader region of which it is part. Its population has risen from an original 21,000 to over 60,000.

The provision by central government of New Town Development Corporations has been but one strand in a hierarchical web of agencies that have provided the context for industrial growth within the county since 1945. Most of the county for much of the time has been covered by development area status of different grades under the Distribution of Industry Acts, in which government-financed industrial estates have been a prominent feature. Here the early momentum of the Team Valley was a decisive factor in its choice in 1960 as the headquarters of the English Industrial Estates Corporation. More recent policies have brought Enterprise Zones and Urban Development Corporations for parts of blighted Tyneside, Wearside and Teesside. There have also been regional agencies: formerly the North East Development and

Washington New Town logo

80

Planning Councils, now the Northern Development Company. Briefly in the mid-1960s there was even a Minister for the North-East. At the two extremes of scale have been the local and county authorities, with their promotional and financial encouragement, and the European and Regional Development Fund, with its grants for roads, industrial estates and visitor projects.

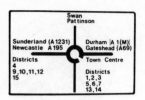

Road sign, Washington New Town

The full impact of this web of administrative support has been masked by the massive decline in employment in mining and heavy manufacturing, with the consequence that the county's unemployment figure has remained well above the national average. Modern manufacturing, moreover, is characteristically capital- rather than labour-intensive. The well-publicised Nissan car assembly plant at Washington, for instance, employs 2,000. In comparative terms this is only half the number who lost their jobs when the Consett works closed or one-third the number employed in the MetroCentre service complex. The latter comparison is perhaps the most relevant one, since the county during the most recent phase of its history has evolved an economy increasingly based on service activities, retailing and tourism.

The most remarkable monument to the post-industrial economy, and one without precedent or roots in the region, is the MetroCentre. The vision belonged to John Hall, the money was that of the Church Commissioners. A significant third element was designation of the area as an Enterprise Zone, with its 10-year freedom from rates. The combination transformed a derelict riverside area three miles west of Gateshead into Europe's biggest 'shopping and leisure experience'. One measure among many to gauge its size is the provision of (free) parking for 10,000 cars.

In addition to the MetroCentre, the northern part of the county also has 'Retail World', developed on a section of the Team Valley Estate, as well as the new Washington Centre. On another large area of derelict land between the Team Valley and the Tyne, on part of the site rejuvenated for the 1990 National Garden Festival, are further leisure facilities. Other possible major leisure projects are a Weardale Ski Centre near Wolsingham and a 1,000-berth yacht marina at the Hartlepools. Meanwhile, the county authority has been active in creating picnic areas and country parks, and converting many disused railway tracks into walkways. At Beamish 300 acres have been laid out since 1970 as the North of England Open Air Museum to retain a record of the county and Tyneside around the turn of the century, when the world was wealth-creating rather than wealth-spending. An adit mine, colliery village, town street and farm are all 'working' environments: the past, we are assured, is 'living', the experience 'authentic'. The same cannot be claimed for 'Catherine Cookson Country' of South Tyneside, which,

81

'Land of the Prince Bishops': the county logo

although the setting of the prolific novelist's works, contains plaques in rose beds to mark the house where she was born, and also her later childhood home. The county authority itself, with its own five-year tourist strategy launched in 1987, viewed the exploitation of history as a key element. Accordingly, all roads entering the county palatine now announce it as the 'Land of the Prince Bishops'. With a prevailing trend to 'theme' development, where fantasy can replace history, care will have to be exercised in order that 1066 does not turn into '1066 and all that'.

The appearance of the county is clearly important in the attraction of visitors, but a programme of environmental improvement long predates the recent emphasis on tourism. The extent of Durham's substandard housing, obsolete industry and despoiled landscapes presented the most formidable post-war restoration challenge to any county in Britain. The authority began its programme before central government funds were available and has restored some 11,000 acres (or 16 square miles) of derelict mining and industrial eyesores, including the levelling of 100 spoilheaps. County financial aid to local authorities resulted in a further 2,300 acres being restored. The transformation has often been remarkable, as Plates 49 and 50 illustrate, although to the trained eye the smoothness of the green contour lacks the unpredictability or ruggedness of the 'natural' northern landscape. In the 1980s the authority deservedly won various awards, including Europa Nostra and Royal Town Planning Institute commendations for its reclamation work.

One direction in which the county's efforts at environmental improvement have been thwarted has been along the coast, where dumping of coal waste into the sea still continues. Until 1939 the sea removed the waste as fast as it was tipped, but increased output from the big coastal pits after 1945 led to waste and black slurry accumulating along, or even forming, the shoreline. Some eight miles of coast are polluted, and dumping continues despite two Royal Commissions and government urging that the practice must cease. Meanwhile, much of the coast is designated by the County Council as a Landscape Improvement Area, along with two broad arms stretching inland across the old coalfield, one towards Consett, the other to Bishop Auckland. The zoning, with its intention of lifting the landscape quality, is to be seen within the scheduling of other tracts of countryside which are already attractive and which are to be protected from inappropriate development (Map 10). Technically, these are either areas of great landscape value (A.G.L.V.) or special landscape value (A.S.L.V.), the latter being smaller. In Tyne and Wear there is no distinction, the more general term 'green belt' being used. The whole of the western half of the county,

82

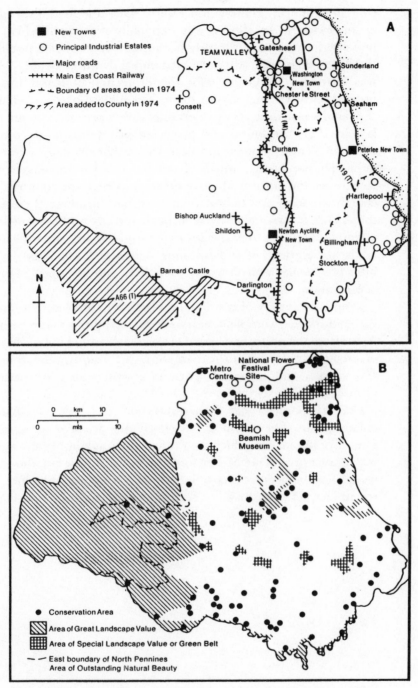

Map 10. Modern County Durham: (a) economic features; (b) social features.

83

consisting of open Pennine moorlands, dales and foothills, is designated as an A.G.L.V. In 1987 it was nationally recognised when, following pressure from the Countryside Commission and after a public inquiry, the North Pennines Area of Outstanding Natural Beauty (A.O.N.B.) was created. The Council for the Protection of Rural England had pressed for its creation in the 1930s. The highest parts are claimed to be 'England's last wilderness'. Certainly rare alpine flora, remnants of the last Ice Age, are found and protected in several nature reserves, but what we term wilderness has been variously exploited by our ancestors for millennia. Today, much of the moorland is 'managed' so that it constitutes the most productive grouse moors in the country. The dales contain some of our richest remaining hay meadows; here farmers in the A.O.N.B. are encouraged through subsidy and informed advice to maintain not only the species-rich meadows but also the traditional landscape features of stone-walling, barns and woodland. Up to two-fifths of a farmer's income may come from subsidy given in the cause of conservation.

While the variety of conservation measures has led to a 'greening' of the countryside, complementary efforts have been made within towns. Apart from the protective listing of several thousand individual buildings of architectural or historical interest, the county now contains over 100 villages and towns, or parts of towns, which are designated as Conservation Areas under the 1967 Civic Amenities Act.

Conservation, no less than restoration, has brought environmental enhancement. The extent of our efforts, the artefacts we value and the attractive manner in which we present them might bring a smile to our recent ancestors. Our earlier forefathers, with little time for aesthetics, would find it incomprehensible. In many respects, therefore, the most recent chapter of history has seen the emergence of a new county.

XIV   Agriculture in County Durham

The history of agriculture in the county strongly reflects the contrast between west and east, between the high moorlands and foothills of the Pennines on the one hand and the lowlands of the rivers Wear and Tees together with the East Durham Plateau on the other. The former, with its greater altitude, higher rainfall and a growing season one to two months shorter than in the lowlands, has the inferior soils. In fact, according to the Ministry of Agriculture, Fisheries and Food's five-fold division of land quality, the thin soils derived from the Millstone Grit and Calcareous Sandstone in the dales and those of the peaty moorlands are classified as the two lowest grades, 4 and 5 respectively. The bulk of the medium to heavy soils in the eastern half of the county, largely derived from glacial drift, are grade 3, with smaller areas of grade 2 confined to the middle Tees west of Darlington and to ones near Durham and Chester-le-Street. (There is no grade 1 land in the county.) This physical background has given rise to a persistent contrast between pastoral activities in the west and arable or mixed farming in the east.

Agricultural systems and related settlement patterns in the county were largely established by the 12th century. In the east were regularly-spaced, small nucleated villages, surrounded by open fields, where the strips and furlongs of scattered holdings were worked communally. Each village or township consisted of 'townfields' of arable, with meadow and pasture intermixed and, beyond, town meadows, pastures and commons. The former was measured in bovates or oxgangs, i.e. the area which one ox could plough and make ready for sowing in one season. Such a unit varied from place to place according to type of soil, but averaged 12 to 15 acres. There was much bondage land, with tied cultivators. Boldon, after which township Bishop Le Puiset's land survey of 1183 is named, provides an example of labour services demanded. Twelve cottagers were registered, from whom work was due two days a week, while 22 villagers owed three days a week, together with carting services and extra labour at times of ploughing, harrowing and harvest, plus dues of oats, hens and eggs.

The dales provided fingers of sheltered lowlands extending into the Pennine moorlands for a few clustered hamlets and isolated farmsteads.

Drystone wall

Here evolved small enclosed fields held in severalty, not communally. A variant of the infield-outfield system operated, the proportion of arable townfield of each township being very small compared with extensive areas of unenclosed and unimproved waste beyond. Pastoralism prevailed, and the land was predominantly exchequer land providing rent for the bishop, although services might be required in the bishop's hunting preserve. In Teesdale, which did not constitute part of the bishop's estate, colonisation was aided by monks from Rievaulx, who were given privileges in the 12th century by Bernard de Baliol (William II had granted much of Teesdale to the Baliols in 1093) for pasture and timber rights, with permanent dwellings provided for lay brothers in assarts (clearings). Here, as in Weardale, the demand for charcoal for local smelting contributed to the wasting of woodland.

The general contrast in land use between east and west at this early date is indicated by the pattern of arable land, calculated from the returns from the surveys of their lands by Bishop Le Puiset and Hatfield (Map 11). Both clearly show higher densities confined to the east. While both surveys cover only lands belonging to the Lord Bishop, the fewer blanks on the later census of Hatfield reflect its more comprehensive nature. The largest proportion of the area left blank on the two maps constituted land belonging to the prior and monastery of Durham, although a few barons also controlled large estates — Brus of Hartlepool, the Baliols and, by the 14th century, most notably the Nevilles of Raby, Brancepeth and Teesdale.

From the western dales there was a steady upward encroachment — with, in Weardale, the bishop's licence — to complete the medieval penetration of the Pennine moorlands. As early as the 13th century effective use was being made of some of the high fells over 2,000 ft. by the seasonal transfer of animals. Circular sheep folds dating from this time are still visible, but evidence suggests that this form of transhumance was less strongly developed than in Westmorland and Northumberland. A related but more extensively developed and flexible system of common pasturing of animals on fell land evolved. It was known as stinting, and became an important component of moorland farming over several centuries. The carrying capacity of stinted pasture was worked out by trial and error through time, with quality of fell or pasture grass, type of animal and demand combining to determine the average price of a stint. Both price and allocation of stints per landowner were calculated annually, at which time stint users had to declare the number and type of livestock that would graze the land. Conversion rates might mean, for instance, that ten stints could support 10 mature cattle, five horses or 25 sheep. Overstinting was prohibited and punishable, with an impounder employed to oversee and seize surplus animals.

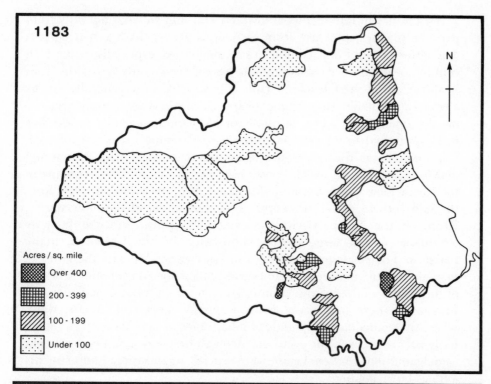

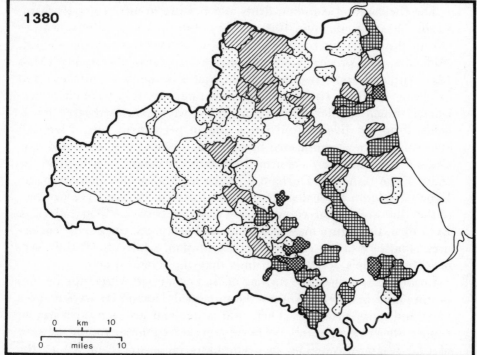

Map 11. Density of arable land in surveys of the bishop's holdings by (a) Le Puiset, 1183; (b) Hatfield, 1380.

Agriculture in late medieval lowland Durham suffered not only from periodic plagues, but also from incursions across the Scottish border. The latter brought devastation to standing crops, especially in the 14th century, while on occasions animals were driven south across the Tees to the safety of the Cleveland Hills. Corn yields were generally low as a result of the slow exhaustion of heavy soils from years of grain growing on the open fields. The ultimate break with this feudal world has been attributed to an external stimulus — London's demand for coal. Certainly it was the emergence of activity connected with the mining and transport of coal which boosted the rise of a capitalistic economy in the North-East. Concomitant political events in the turbulent years from the mid-16th to mid-17th centuries — dissolution of the monasteries, Rising of the North, Civil War, Commonwealth, and the Jacobite Rebellion — saw large estates confiscated by the Crown in many parishes. The consequent changes in land ownership saw the entry of new, mercantile families. An important factor for an economic working of the land was the introduction of short-term leases at a realistic rent. Previously there had been the widespread custom of 'tenant right' whereby tenants had copyholds of inheritance at nominal rent in return for border services in the event of a Scottish invasion. Land engrossment (amalgamation) and enclosure were crucial organisational adjustments among farm holdings.

The enclosure of common fields and pasture to form compact farmsteads began in the mid-16th century, but was especially a feature late in the following century, well ahead of enclosure in the English Midlands. The process was confined to the east of the county (Map 12a). Although some two-fifths of enclosures in the two centuries up to 1750 concerned the enclosure of common pasture, they were characteristically much smaller than the majority, which enclosed large town-fields, formerly divided into strips and in permanent cultivation. All enclosures were accomplished by agreement among the interested parties, although half were confirmed by chancery decree — usually in the court of the bishop of Durham — often to legalise the division made. Robert Hodgson has calculated that at least 75,000 acres (12 per cent of the total area of the county) were enclosed between 1550 and 1750. Even then, this figure may well be an underestimate since some enclosures almost certainly escaped documentation, while others were recorded in bishop's acres, larger units than the standard acre.

Barn, Middle End Farm, Teesdale

Enclosure permitted the turning of land exhausted with cropping into pasture land in order to supply the increased demand for wool and for meat and dairy products. There was a demand also for extra hay to support the growing number of horses who served the spreading network of coal wagon-ways. The new emphasis on pastoralism led to the

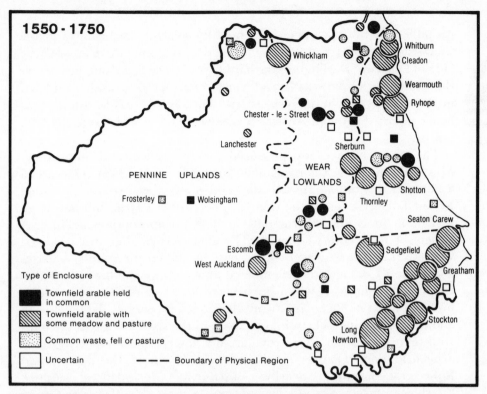

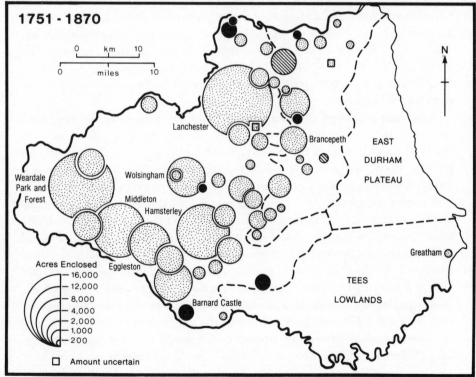

Map 12.   Enclosures in County Durham: (a) 1550-1750; (b) 1751-1870. (After Hodgson.)

Durham ox, 1790

dwindling or disappearance of some fifty villages, particularly in the south-eastern quarter of the county. At the same time there arose cattle fairs in Durham, Darlington, Barnard Castle, Sedgefield and, just across the boundary, in Newcastle and Yarm. Dairy produce was stimulated in the vicinity of the largest centres, notably Newcastle. Butter was being exported through Newcastle and Stockton by the end of the 17th century.

The era of change also produced its own agricultural 'improvers'. Most prominent was George Culley, born at Denton in 1734, who earned a national reputation. He and his brother Matthew, who both visited Robert Bakewell, learnt the trade on their father's farm, but had to go to Fenton in Northumberland to acquire an appropriate holding. A variety of innovations followed. The efforts of another two brothers, whose farming careers were spent entirely within the county, Charles and Robert Colling, are remembered above all for the breeding of the Durham shorthorn. It was a beast noted for its sturdiness and yield of beef and milk; its sheer size meant that much fat was available for soap and candle making. The initial increase in the size of cattle in the mid-18th century is said to have come from a few Friesians imported to the Sedgefield area. Charles (at Ketton, just north of Darlington) and Robert (at Barmpton, nearby) subsequently proceeded by selective breeding to produce prodigiously heavy animals. The 'Durham Ox' of Charles and the 'White Heifer' of Robert were both taken on tour around England at the beginning of the 19th century as wonders of the age (Plate 41). The transport of the heavy beasts — the 'Durham Ox' weighed 270 stone — in special carts was no mean feat. They were immortalised in contemporary engravings and prints, and also in the naming of hostelries.

A second phase of enclosure in the county began in the mid-18th century. It complemented the irony of the earlier phase on the lowland eastern half of the county, when enclosing of arable townfields gave a boost to pastoralism. Now, upland fell enclosure somewhat surprisingly brought about an increase in cereal production. Grain prices had risen throughout the 18th century from the demand of an increasing industrial population; during the Napoleonic Wars the cost of importing grain rose dramatically. As a result, the upland areas were viewed for their potential contribution to this market. On the more suitable commons of the foothill zone, the newly-enclosed land was rented and leased for up to ten times its former value and put under the plough. Relict patterns of ridge and furrow, such as those above Wolsingham and St John's Chapel, however, are lasting evidence that barley and oats were widely grown at altitudes of 1-1,200 ft. Part-time farming, undertaken for subsistence or standby among an increasing number of

90

leadminers, contributed to what today appears as either optimistic or foolhardy cultivation.

The process of enclosure from the mid-18th century contrasts markedly with the earlier period not only in its western distribution and husbandry. It was achieved not by individual agreement but through Parliamentary acts and awards, many of which covered very extensive areas. Enclosure of Lanchester Common and Weardale Park both involved more than 15,000 acres; Wolsingham was more than 10,000; several others exceeded 2,000 acres (Map 12b). Altogether over 110,000 acres, or some 17 per cent of the county, were enclosed in the period 1750-1870, all but a mere 5,000 involving common, moor, fell or waste. It is from this time that the landscape of the western half of the county received its distinctive mantle of stone-walling, aligned in a regular grid-pattern up hill and across fell (Plate 40).

The provision of a mosaic of compact, more manageable holdings was not accompanied by a commensurate advance in husbandry techniques which the new organisational framework might have suggested. In his *Tour* of 1769 Arthur Young had summarised Durham agriculture, apart from a few large, well-managed units, as simple and primitive. Bailey drew the same distinction in his *General Account of Agriculture* in 1810. Innovation was confined to the educated managers of a few large farms; the majority, particularly those on short-lease holdings, still persisted with the traditional and monotonous rotation of two crops and bare fallow. There was no proper appreciation of preserving soil fertility, to the extent that most arable ground often received only lime, apart from lying fallow, while at the same time manure might be stacked on pasture land. In short, there was no beneficial integration of crop and livestock. The Crop Returns of 1801, with the dominance of traditional grains and restricted coverage of turnips and potatoes, are a statistical confirmation of Bailey's observations. The livestock itself was provided with inadequate accommodation on most farms. Lack of capital was a handicap to small farmers, whose lives, according to Bailey, was onerous to the extent that he deemed them 'greater slaves than their servants'.

Bell, in his mid-century review of the county's agriculture, repeated some of the same points, by which time a further handicap to efficient agriculture was evident. According to Bell there was not a parish in the county that was not scarred from mining — of lead in the west and coal elsewhere. Over large areas colliery owners either bought or farmed land, in order to avoid meeting claims for surface damage and compensation for loss of crops from tenant farmers. Where paid, compensation often provided a return twice the rental or commercial value of the land — hardly an incentive for dedicated farming. However, the rapid spread of mining in the second half of the 19th century did provide an incentive for hay and oats production in order to support the growing number of pit ponies. The colliery districts also provided a market for pigs, which were fattened in the backyards of miners' cottages before ritual slaughter and a shared distribution of cuts among neighbouring families. The miners themselves also provided their own form of market gardening on the edge of pit villages. Their allotments, notable for the distinctive architecture of sheds and pigeon lofts, also became the basis for fruit and vegetable competitions, not least in the growing of leeks. Durham County Agricultural Society, founded in 1786, encouraged competition on a wider basis.

The second half of the century saw a decline in wheat acreage, which was more than offset by a rise in pasture and meadow for increased cattle numbers. Earlier there had been the decline in and cessation of cultivation of two specialised crops. Mustard had been grown only for a relatively short period following the country's first manufacture of the condiment in Durham City in the late 17th century. Flax, on the other hand, had a long history of cultivation, and was the basis of linen manufacture in several towns. For a brief period towards the end of the late 18th century, the concentration of mills in Darlington along the Skerne was the largest of any town in England. Symptomatic of its position was the patent for a water-driven flax spinner applied for by John Kendrew of Darlington in 1787. The yarn was dispatched to weavers in Durham, Cumberland and Yorkshire. In the first part of the 19th century, however, the greater textile resources of West Yorkshire were exploited, while Darlington entrepreneurs, with Quaker influence prominent, turned to other manufactures.

The present century has seen an increasing application of science to farming, the most obvious summary index of its success being reflected in the reduction of workers engaged in agriculture. At the beginning of the 19th century the eighteen thousand employed full-time in agriculture formed by far the leading occupation group; a hundred years later the figure had declined by a quarter. Today under 6,000 — 1.2 per cent of the total — earn their living from the land. Cereal cultivation, with its progressive mechanisation, had spearheaded this trend. Horse-drawn reaping machinery was introduced in the 1870s and binders in the 1890s. The mechanisation of threshing began earlier, in 1875, when the first mill was powered by a harnessed horse walking a circular path to drive a thresher in an adjacent barn. Circular wheelsheds which housed these former 'horse-gins' remain a distinctive feature of many lowland farms. Steam power was widely applied by mid-century; mobile threshers, drawn by traction engines, came into use before the end of the century.

The present century has also seen two new land uses in the west of the county — forest plantations and reservoirs. The former, predominantly

Gin-gang, Beamish

33. Shipbuilding at Southwick, Sunderland, 1859. A painting by D. F. McLea.

34. The North Dock of Seaham Harbour in the mid-1870s, crowded with colliers.

35. The launch of the *John Bowes* at Jarrow in 1852.

36. The Butter Market at Barnard Castle, *c*.1890.

37. Barnard Castle before the demolition of the mills. This photograph was taken in the 1920s.

38. Bishop Auckland market, *c.*1900.

39. Bondgate, Darlington, *c.*1890.

40. Aerial view of part of Lanchester Fell, enclosed in the 1780s.

41. Charles Colling's famous 'Durham Ox'.

of spruce and larch, are the work of the Forestry Commission from 1919. Hamsterley Forest in Weardale is the most extensive plantation. In contrast, Teesdale, apart from Egglestone parish, has withstood the Commission's advances. The explanation lies in land ownership and the policy of the Raby and Strathmore estates, which have continued to foster pastoral activities in the dale and maintain higher moorland for sheep and grouse. A dozen reservoirs have been built to trap the headwaters of western valleys. By far the biggest are the two most recent constructions — Derwent (1967), on a tributary of the Tyne, and Cow Green (1970) on the Tees. Around the margin of the former, more land has been taken for picnic areas and a yachting centre. The damming of the Tees just above Cauldron Snout was achieved after a public inquiry. Controversy raged, not because the area was valuable agriculturally but unique botanically, being part of the Teesdale assemblage on Widdybank Fell of alpine and arctic flora, survivors of the last Ice Age.

A recent aspect of land use competition is the intertwining of agriculture and mining for a second time on the exposed part of the coalfield. In some instances it is only a few years since the land has been physically restored from colliery workings and reclaimed for agriculture. A second wave, this time of open-cast workings, requires whole areas to be taken out of production and the land stripped to expose the seams beneath. History is also repeating itself in that farmers may well be anxious to accept the compensation offered rather than continue to work what may be marginal land in the present context of national — and international — quotas and restrictions.

Despite the increasing scientific application to all aspects of production, and despite changes in scale and context, the basic physical endowment of the county has ensured that the contrast between east and west is as strong as at the time of the first colonisation when, according to an early monk of Durham, the county was released from being 'nothing but a hiding place for wild and woodland beasts'. A pastoral west and a mixed arable and stock-rearing east are the basis for the simple arrangement of land use: two-fifths of the county which is in tillage and temporary grass is predominantly in the east; the one-fifth in rough grazing is entirely in the west; the two fifths in permanent grass is shared.

Barn, Headlam, Teesdale

93

XV   The Architectural Face

The present architectural face of the county is a palimpsest: the visible record of the victorious, the powerful and the wealthy. Military and ecclesiastical contributions were to the fore initially; later came civil and industrial elements, followed by widespread residential growth. During this story the Union of the crowns of England and Scotland in 1603 was a significant landmark, for the freedom from border warfare heralded the possibility of a prosperous eonomy and confidence in architectural expression. The county itself possessed a variety of materials with which the appearance might be fashioned, and it was only after the advent of rail transport that the traditional correspondence between appearance and underlying geology was loosened.

All the major geological divisions within the county have provided local building stone — from the grey-white Carboniferous Limestone of the west, succeeded eastwards by the dull grey of the Millstone Grit, the buff or golden brown of the Coal Measure sandstones to the creamy Magnesian Limestone which extends to the coast. Red Triassic sandstone offers further variety in the extreme south-east of the county (see Map 1). Colour apart, the texture of the architectural face is determined by whether the stone has been laid as uncoursed, coursed or squared rubble or in ashlar blocks. The first two are the most common, the last reserved for the more important constructions. Weathering also plays its part. The Triassic sandstone is very soft and weathers easily. The ancient churches of Billingham and Norton bear witness to this fact, but even the extensively used Coal Measure sandstone, depending on quarry and cut of stone, may suffer badly from weathering. Even Durham Castle and Cathedral are not immune in this respect; the mere passage of air can honeycomb stone protected from obvious assault of outside elements, as the castle crypt chapel and cathedral cloister reveal.

In view of the abundance of stone, the use of wood for timber-framed constructions remained relatively unimportant. Brickmaking on any scale was a late feature for the same reason. Roofing slates or flags — at least on the most important buildings — were also provided by the same geology. Gritstone was common in the west, sandstone in the east. On some buildings only the lowest courses were in flagstone, the bulk of the roof being covered with straw or heather thatch, but most roofs were originally covered entirely in thatch. This, though prone to fire and vermin, was nevertheless more thermally effective than flags — or clay pantiles, which became widespread in the east of the county during the 18th century. These various materials laid the foundation for the present scene.

The earliest architecture in the county must be attributed to the Romans, although its appreciation today has to be largely archaeological. The excavations at Binchester and South Shields, the latter with a reconstructed West gate, enable one to begin to acknowledge the building expertise of the invading civilisation. The quality of their stonework is also visible in a few later Anglo-Saxon buildings where Roman sites were used as quarries for the later constructions. This is most clearly seen at Escomb, where the large stones — some five ft. long — constituting the walls of the seventh-century church were brought from the nearby fort at Binchester. The characteristic Roman diamond broaching, or cross-hatching, is widely visible; on one stone there is a Roman inscription referring to the Sixth Legion. Stones forming the present nave of St Mary's church, Seaham, are similarly thought to have come from a nearby signal station.

Escomb church is the least altered of the surviving Anglo-Saxon churches in the county. In consequence, it best illustrates their compact form, narrowly rectangular, with tall walls punctuated by a few small windows high up, and with a steeply pitched roof (Plate 7). The same proportions can be appreciated at St Paul's, Jarrow, where the present chancel formed the nave of the original church. The walls also illustrate what contemporary stonemasons could achieve without the advantage of Roman pre-cut stone (Plate 5). Later Saxon churches, such as those at Hart and Heighington, were broader in relation to length, but Norton is the only example of a cruciform plan. The Saxon tower is best illustrated at the twin monasteries of Jarrow and Monkwearmouth and, in the south of the county, at Billingham and Staindrop.

Several churches illustrate aspects of the solidity of the succeeding Norman Romanesque — the west tower at Kelloe, chancel at Lanchester, nave pillar and arcading at Pittington. Others appear equally illustrative, but are in fact 19th-century rebuildings. Croxdale, Sherburn Hospital and St Mary-the-Less in Durham are the most complete examples. The purest and most authentic Norman ecclesiastical architecture is, of course, in the castle crypt chapel (Plate 11) and the cathedral in Durham. Although separated by a mere 300 yards, they are greatly contrasted buildings. The chapel is early (1072) and embedded in the castle mound. Its six circular pillars with grotesquely carved capitals support low vaulting over narrow central and side aisles. The

Norman doorway,
St Andrew's church,
Dalton-le-Dale

cathedral rises majestically skywards and reveals a change in scale and detail from the chancel and nave (1093-1133) to the Galilee chapel (1175) at the west end (Plates 12 and 13). Its architectural pre-eminence stems from it containing the three main elements that announced the dawn of the Gothic era — flying buttresses, supporting ribbed vaulting and pointed arches. It was at Durham that the thrust problem was resolved and a large building was completely vaulted in stone — one of the great discoveries of European civilisation.

Norman ecclesiastical architecture hardly extended to monastic houses because of the tight Benedictine rule from Durham, which priory, however, established county seats at Muggleswick, Bearpark, Pittington and at Finchale (Plate 19). Enough of the last-named's walls remain to appreciate its mid-13th-century character.

It is not surprising that evidence of military architecture is present in this former border one. Although there are few remains of pele towers, unlike Northumberland, a line of seven castles was strung diagonally across the lowland part of the county (Map 13a). Others at Stockton, Bishop Middleham and Bishopton have completely disappeared. The seven can be broadly divided into curtain-walled military strongholds and fortified houses. The division is attributable to age. The earliest two, Durham and Barnard Castle, defended major routeways through the Wear lowlands and Teesdale, respectively, and both are prominently sited on rocky promontories above major rivers. Durham was rebuilt in stone from 1072 on the orders of William I as his northern stronghold. The motte and bailey and series of enclosing walls can be traced today, while the original Norman imprint is gloriously visible in the northern range, despite its subsequent subdivision.

Barnard Castle was begun soon after Durham by Guy de Baliol on land given by William II, but rebuilt in the middle of the 12th century by his nephew, Bernard Baliol, after whom castle and town are named (Plate 14). Much of the walling, which encloses 6 acres, dates from this period; the 50-ft. high keep was reconstructed in 1300 on its Norman foundation. The present ruinous shell dates from the early 17th century, when Sir Henry Vane purchased the castle and partially dismantled it in order to restore his second purchase, Raby Castle (Plate 20). Both had belonged to the Neville family for some four centuries, but were forfeited to the Crown as a result of their stand during the Rising of the North.

Raby Castle, first mentioned in the 11th century and reputedly the palace of Canute, is substantially a 14th-century structure, with a notable pillared Lower Hall (1325). With its numerous towers, an appearance of antiquity has been maintained throughout subsequent alterations by John Carr and James Paine in the 18th century and

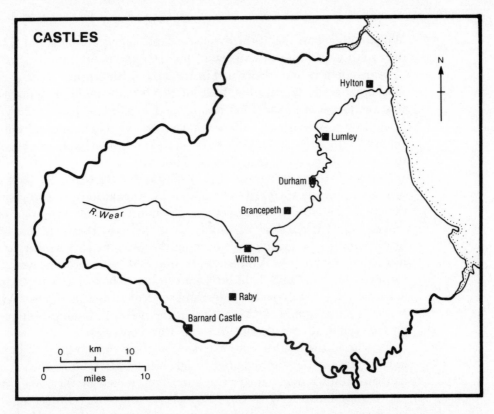

CASTLES

Hylton

Lumley

Durham

Brancepeth

R. Wear

Witton

Raby

Barnard Castle

0 km 10

0 miles 10

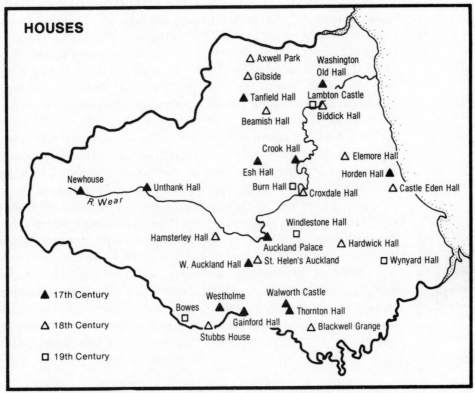

HOUSES

△ Axwell Park

△ Gibside

Washington
Old Hall ▲

▲ Tanfield Hall

Lambton Castle □ △

△ Beamish Hall

Biddick Hall

Crook Hall ▲

△ Elemore Hall

Esh Hall ▲

Horden Hall ▲

Newhouse ▲

R. Wear

▲ Unthank Hall

Burn Hall □

Croxdale Hall △

△ Castle Eden Hall

Windlestone Hall □

Hamsterley Hall △

▲ Auckland Palace

△ Hardwick Hall

W. Auckland Hall ▲ △ St. Helen's Auckland

□ Wynyard Hall

▲ 17th Century

Bowes □

Westholme ▲

Walworth Castle ▲

Thornton Hall ▲

△ 18th Century

△ Stubbs House

Gainford Hall ▲

△ Blackwell Grange

□ 19th Century

Map 13. (a) Castles and (b) great houses in the county.

William Burns in the 19th. Extensive landscaped grounds and a large deer herd contribute to its present picturesque quality.

Brancepeth is first mentioned in the early 13th century when it came into the Neville family, but little of the Neville building remains. It too was forfeited in the 1569 Rising, and in the late 18th century was bought by a Sunderland banker and coal owner. The castle was entirely rebuilt by John Paterson after 1817 on a grand, if forbidding scale, with distinctive 'chessmen' gate towers (Plate 15).

Lumley Castle was constructed in the 14th century to a compact plan around a central courtyard, with massive towers at the four corners. The display of heraldic shields over the gatehouse denotes the pride of its owners, the ancient Lumley family. It is the most complete late castle in the county, the basic plan surviving the gracious 18th-century transformations by Sir John Vanbrugh. Hylton and Witton castles were both fortified about the middle of the 15th century. The former's rectangular construction was relatively modest and referred to as a gatehouse. Witton presents a traditional curtain wall, but the present buildings were much enlarged and altered in the 18th and 19th centuries.

In general the castles were extended as their owners grew in importance, and were transformed increasingly into comfortable country houses as their military role waned. The latter fact, sealed by the 1603 Union, and accompanied by growing prosperity in the 17th century, heralded the first significant strand of domestic architecture. (Crook Hall, Durham, with its 14th-century hall and kitchen, is the only substantially complete manor house from an earlier period.) The 17th century saw the construction of many moderate-sized stone manor houses and farmhouses (Map 13b). Gainford Hall (1603), the earliest, set a happy precedent with its formal symmetry and elegance. Its builder was the vicar of Gainford, the Rev. John Cradock, who was obviously alert to Renaissance design. Of the other manor houses, Washington Old Hall is of interest. 'Old' because it was superseded by another in the 19th century, the Old Hall itself had incorporated part of the original medieval house. Some thick walling is the clue to the original house, which for two centuries was home to the ancestors of George Washington.

Bishop James had been responsible for the building of Washington Old Hall. Another bishop, Cosin, was responsible for the internal refurbishment of numerous churches. His exuberant woodwork is a distinctive feature of the county's architecture. From the 1630s, when he was rector of Brancepeth, and then, after interruption, as the first Restoration bishop in the 1660s, there was an active programme to replace in vigorous Renaissance style the woodwork lost in the Reformation — screens, stalls, pews, pulpits, panelling, ceilings, font covers, and so on. Of the parish churches enriched, Brancepeth, Sedgefield,

Washington Old Hall

98

Houghton le Skerne (Darlington) and Egglescliffe are particularly fine. His chapel at Bishop Auckland and the cathedral were embellished on a grand scale. His Black Staircase in Durham Castle is a remarkable construction. Nearby, in quieter vein, his Library conveys a dignified charm. In the city of Durham itself there was a blossoming of woodworking. Although actual timber-framed constructions were few — but not as rare as generally believed — Francis Johnson has dated nearly three dozen extant wooden staircases of late Stuart type. Although varying in elegance, they are characterised by a spaciousness in contrast with the early, defensively-designed newel stair.

An increasing emphasis on elegance, both internal and external, signified — in Ronald Brunskill's terms — an architecture that is polite rather than vernacular. Its hallmarks are professional designers, incorporation of national or international rules and use of materials for stylistic effect as well as utility. Most buildings, however, continued to be vernacular in origin, using local materials in a traditional manner, and were designed and erected by architects and builders who were perhaps untaught and whose names have been forgotten. The less accessible western half of the county was naturally the area where such a mode lasted longest. Among farm buildings, Brunskill has shown that the typical longhouse of the North Pennines did not cross Stainmore into Durham. Here, although the common farmhouse was a simple elongated one with byre attached, there was no interconnection. Cottages for labourers in field or in mine remained essentially one-room dwellings until well into the 18th century.

The increasing prosperity of the 18th century brought embellishment of existing castles and the appearance of a few new mansions, often with extensively landscaped grounds, in which other buildings might be set. Classicism was the prevailing style for much of the century, with the Palladian architecture of Axwell Park by James Paine considered perhaps the finest example. Paine also built Bradley Hall, as well as garden buildings and the chapel at Gibside. The last-named was begun in 1760 to the plan of a Greek cross with projecting arms, the remarkable quality of the stone matching its perfect proportions. Other notable halls are those at Croxdale, Elemore and Biddick. The taste for Gothick — the 'k', as it were, denoting the light-heartedness of the decorative style — which began during the second half of the 18th century, brought fashion merely to parts of the great houses. Other buildings on their estates might be wholly essays in the new Gothick — a gatehouse at Auckland, for instance, a pavilion (at Raby), a bridge (Hardwick), or a deerhouse (Auckland).

Entrance, Bishop Auckland Castle

The second half of the 18th century was an era of landscape gardening. Grounds of great houses were designed, increasingly on principles of the

99

picturesque, with water, hills, trees and buildings arranged to provide many pleasing prospects. At Hardwick Hall, John Burden spent so much on landscaping his 300-acre park with lake, serpentine canal and seven buildings that there was no money left to erect the centre-piece, a mansion designed for him by James Paine. The most complete land-scaped parkland was at Gibside, laid out to the design of its owner, George Bowes, a coal magnate. Here, apart from banqueting hall, orangery and stables, the eye-catching components at either end of a long tree-lined avenue are the 140-ft. high Column of British Liberty and the chapel. In Durham City the river gorge assumed its park function at this time.

Among 18th-century gardeners, James Paine was the most active in the county. Capability Brown, although born in neighbouring Northumberland, apparently did no work in Durham. On the other hand, Thomas Wright (1711-86) from Byers Green near Bishop Auckland, whom historians view as a director of public taste in the interlude between William Kent and Brown, and who was involved in some dozen gardens in the south and midlands, designed merely a 'concatonation of cataracts' for the grounds at Raby in his own county. Apart, that is, from his own garden and villa at Byers Green, so aligned to frame views of the river Wear and distant Durham Cathedral. Sadly, neither villa nor garden remain, although nearby the gates at the entrance to Auckland Park at Park Head are to his design. At Westerton Hill his round Gothick observatory tower is a reminder that he won fame as an astronomer as well as being gardener and architect.

Certain towns still reflect in their architecture the expansion of 18th-century prosperity. Barnard Castle in particular, an important market and woollen textile centre at this time, is lined with stone-built, three-storey weavers' houses and handsome town houses, which focus on the market cross and octagonal town hall of 1747 (Plates 36 and 37). Town houses for county families also appeared in Durham City during this period, while brick rather than stone became the fashion, a trend that had been growing for nearly a century. The earliest extant brickwork in the county — in Durham Castle, dated 1499 — was considerably in advance of any general use. Stockton parish church, built in 1712, was the first substantial civic building in brick. Together with a new Town House (1735), Market Cross (1765) and Customs House (1730, demolished 1969), it reflected Stockton's prosperity as a port and market centre (Plate 21). In the north of the county, the industrial and port trade of South Shields was captured in its Town Hall (1768) and St Hilda's church (1764). The county's fastest growing centre, Sunderland, has left only its parish church, Holy Trinity (1719), as a legacy. The most remarkable symbol of its advance, an iron bridge (1796) over the incised

Observatory tower, Westerton

mouth of the Wear, was dismantled in 1929. Designed by Rowland
Burdon of Castle Eden, the elegant cast-iron single span was double
the length, but significantly lighter, than the world's first at Ironbridge
17 years earlier.

Town halls are a good indicator of economic success during the 19th
century when railways often provided the vital stimulant. Civic pride
in the town's success is shown in Durham (1851), Darlington (1864),
Gateshead (1868), Bishop Auckland (1869), Sunderland (1887, now
demolished), West Hartlepool (1893), followed by Jarrow (1902) and
South Shields (1905). Appropriately, Durham, the earliest, and the town
least stimulated by rail transport, was built in modest Perpendicular; the
remainder were more notable piles, largely in Victorian Gothic.

*Sunderland Old Town
Hall (1890)*

As channels of economic life, railways focused activity at ports. At
Seaham Harbour and West Hartlepool the arrival of the railway called
forth plans for new towns. At the former, John Dobson's imaginative
classical design of the 1820s for Lord Londonderry's town was unfortunately delayed and then largely neglected as resources were diverted
towards construction and expansion of the harbour for the export of coal.
At West Hartlepool, the grid pattern of central streets and prominent
buildings (customs house and dock offices, warehouse, church, masonic
lodge, athenaeum and hotel) still speak strongly of the mid-Victorian
prosperity promoted by Ralph Wood Jackson.

Railways themselves brought their own contribution to the architectural mosaic of the county. Darlington, appropriately, has the most
imposing monument, where its Bank Top Station (1887) is enclosed by
high tunnel-vaulting; outside, its clock tower rivals that of a town hall.
A few hundred yards from Bank Top, on the old North Eastern Railway,
is North Road Station (1842), which was on the Stockton and Darlington
Railway. The simple Georgian building is now a museum. Some of the
county's viaducts also combine architectural elegance with engineering
skill, most noticeably in the stone and brick structure at Houns Gill
(1858, Sir Thomas Bouch) and in Durham City (1857, Robert Stephenson).

Nineteenth-century success is expressed in the few great country
mansions, most notably in Wynyard Park and Lambton Castle, homes
of the two leading coal magnates, the Londonderry and Lambton
families, respectively. The classical grandeur of Wynyard stems from
the fact that it was built in the 1820s to the design of a palace intended
for the Duke of Wellington, who was a close friend of the third marquis.
The design was borrowed, and executed by Philip Wyatt. When fire
gutted most of the building in 1841, it was reconstructed on original
lines by Ignatius Bonomi.

At the same time that Wynyard was arising, the family home of the

101

Lambtons was being partially encased, mightily extended and generally given the appearance of a castle, by Bonomi. Here, mining subsidence brought about a partial rebuilding to plans by John Dobson in 1862. Much of this rebuilding was pulled down in the 1930s. The extensive grounds of both houses were laid out with customary verve, and with contents that befitted the owners.

Two other notable 19th-century mansions, Burn Hall and Windle-stone Hall, were both designed by Bonomi. Born in London of Italian descent, and working for forty years from his Durham office, Ignatius Bonomi (1789-1870) was unrivalled as an architect within the county. His better-known contemporary classicist, John Dobson (1787-1865), while supreme north of the Tyne, was less successful in County Durham, where no complete major project remains. Bonomi was County Bridge Surveyor from 1813 and Architect to the Cathedral from 1828. Although best known for his Greek Classical designs, he was adept at building in his client's desired style, and Bonomi's versatility was illustrated by his varied output — churches, mansions, artisan housing, assize courts, institutes and bridges.

Gothic revival, as opposed to classicism, characterised a second archi-tect with strong Durham connections, named Anthony Salvin (1799-1881). Although born in the south, and practising from his London office, he was a member of the ancient Salvin family of Sunderland Bridge, two miles south of Durham City. He spent most of his youth in the county, with relatives at Willington and attending Durham School. It was at nearby Brancepeth that he was engaged as a pupil by John Paterson during the massive rebuilding of the castle. Salvin's interest in medieval architecture was confirmed, and at the age of 25 he was elected a Fellow of the Society of Antiquaries, by which time he was in London and had just embarked on the first of his commissions to restore castles and churches. In Durham City restoration was carried out at cathedral, castle (including rebuilding the keep) and university library. Nearby he built Hatfield College, an observatory and obelisk and a master's house for his old school; beyond, he built churches in South Shields, Darlington and Shildon.

Quite the most remarkable piece of grand architecture of 19th-century Durham — Bowes Museum, on the outskirts of Barnard Castle — was designed by a Frenchman, Jules Pellechet. Its use is not a subsequent conversion, for this enormous French Renaissance chateau, complete with formal gardens and fountains, was intended from the beginning to be a museum and art gallery for the Bowes — John and his French wife, Josephine. England rather than France was chosen for their project be-cause of the political unrest in the latter country; Barnard Castle was chosen as the site since the estate was near the family home at Streatlam. The chateau was begun in 1869 and took 23 years to complete (Plate 18).

A second remarkable enterprise that owed its origin to events in France is the Roman Catholic seminary of Ushaw College, a prominent Gothic complex situated high on the crest between the Deerness and Browney valleys, four miles west of Durham. Refugees from the French Revolution settled here at the beginning of the century. The Pugins, senior and junior, designed much of the earlier part, including the chapel, while a much taller and larger chapel for the expanding college was built by Dunn and Hansom in 1884.

The 19th century brought an explosion of urban residential architecture, most of it terraced and much subsequently replaced this century. Streets of generously-proportioned classical terraces remain in the larger towns, however, especially Sunderland. The Esplanade and adjoining terraces, now part of the Ashbrooke Conservation Area, illustrate their elegance. Sunderland was also unusual for its central streets of single-storey terraced cottages, some of which have withstood the advances of modern developers. Darlington provides the clearest example of classical villa development, where early Quakers and subsequent imitators created a distinctive western quarter.

Outside towns the most widespread feature was the replication of mean urban designs in dozens of pit villages. Housing in the earliest was sometimes built of stone, but soon brick became universal. The bricks for the cottages in the parallel colliery rows were often made on site from shale and clay procured from the mine itself. Each individual brick might therefore bear the imprint of the colliery company, indicating a thousand-fold the all-pervasiveness of the tied housing.

The 20th century has seen more building than all the previous centuries put together; much of it is residential and much in materials and styles found throughout the country. From the time of the First World War until the 1950s, however, the depressed economy severely curtailed building and any architectural expression. Some of the physical repercussions accompanying the economic fall and rise have been mentioned in previous chapters, so attention will be focused here on the major features.

During the inter-war period the chemical industry of Billingham added a new and even more dramatic skyline to the county with its maze of steel cylinders, pipes and chimneys. In contrast, conventional brick and garden city densities were incorporated in William Holford's design for the Team Valley Trading Estate in 1936, with factories lining a long tree-lined avenue. Industrial estates of the post-war county have often adopted the warehouse model: curtain walling in metal. The recent extensive Nissan car-assembly plant, alongside the A19 between Washington and Sunderland, has adopted this same functional design. A similar appearance is presented by recent trading estates, which, again, are located and laid out for the car-borne. Nationally-recognised logos and colourful facades hardly conceal their basic construction. 'Retail World' on the Team Valley Estate is the clearest example. Retailing is to the fore in the MetroCentre, which is the biggest single project in the county. It was designed to be experienced from the air-conditioned interior, where eclectic stylistic borrowing and modern finishes have conjured a complete and amazing illusion. The new world within, however, has been created at the expense of the real world without, which is devoted to an extensive surrounding tarmac apron for car parking.

More conventional architecture is found in at least two of the county's three New Towns, Newton Aycliffe and Peterlee, although the latter retains hints of the briefly promised spectacular architecture. Grenfell Bains and Hargreaves drew up the Master Plan for both towns, based on strict land use zoning and residential neighbourhoods. The Master Plan of Washington New Town, produced by Llewelyn-Davies, Weeks and Partners, two decades later, was much more flexible in layout and use, and more reliant on a car-owning population to use its highway network. All three New Town Corporations, having completed their work, have been superseded by a New Town Commission.

Among towns with a longer — and particularly active 19th-century — history, the texture and townscape of the inner areas has often been destroyed since the 1950s, to be replaced by the sweep of new roads and studded with systems-built tower blocks. The centres of Sunderland and Gateshead especially have suffered in this way. Distinctive individual buildings in central positions have been built for administration and leisure. Billingham Forum (Elder Lester and Partners, 1958) and the Crowtree Leisure Centre, Sunderland (Gillingson, Barnett and Partners, 1978) are both fun palaces beneath space-frame roofs. Three civic centres — no longer merely town halls — at Darlington (1970), Sunderland (1970) and Chester-le-Street (1982) are each quite different in concept. Contrast, for instance, the heavy hexagonal design in brick by Sir Basil Spence at Sunderland, with the light spinal, barrel-vaulted arcade in glass and aluminium by Faulkner Brown and Partners at Chester-le-Street.

The most varied collection of modern architecture, much of it highly creditable, is in Durham City. Apart from a new County Hall, appropriately designed by the county architects in municipal idiom in 1963, the expanding university has been patron for 10 award-winning constructions — colleges, library, lecture theatres, union building and its own bridge. In the centre of the city, respect for the historic setting shown by

104

a large shopping centre (Building Design Partnership, 1976) won it a Europa Nostra Award. Moreover, there can be few cities in the country where a multi-storey carpark (William Whitfield, 1975) is faced with high-quality brick and even some natural stone. But then, Durham City is unique. It is appropriate, therefore, to turn to the county town to conclude our history.

Observatory, Durham

XVI   The City of Durham

The story of the city, no less than of the county, begins with Cuthbert, a shepherd boy from the Borders who became bishop of Lindisfarne (Holy Island). He was a saintly man in his lifetime and a legend after his death in 687; many miracles were subsequently associated with his name. Two centuries after his death, his followers, now the 'Cuthbert Community', left Lindisfarne in the face of Viking raids, taking with them the body of their saint, and valuables, together with the community's privileges, to settle in Chester-le-Street. A century later the community became peripatetic once more with the threat of further raids, and wandered as far south as Ripon. They were possibly on their way back to Chester-le-Street in 995 when they were attracted to the defensive qualities of the flat-topped, steep-sided plateau area within the meander loop of the Wear six miles south of their former home. There was already Saxon settlement on a river terrace under the brow of the hill, Aelfret ee ('Swan Island', the present Elvet), but it was Dunholm ('hill island') which was selected as the site on which to erect a cathedral worthy to contain the shrine of St Cuthbert. The building was completed in 1017 and the plateau area fortified. The addition of the remains of the Venerable Bede, brought from the monastery of Jarrow in 1022, increased its attraction. King Canute was among the early pilgrims; he granted extensive tracts of land and other privileges to the community.

The site chosen for St Cuthbert was mightily confirmed by the conquering Normans. In a strategic buffer zone on the east coast lowland route to Scotland, the recent Saxon fortifications on a naturally defensible peninsula had already been proved in withstanding two attacks from Scottish armies. William therefore chose Durham, rather than his 'new castle' on the Tyne 14 miles north, as the centre of Norman administration in northern England, and thus the name of Dunholm, the hill island, was assigned to the surrounding countryside. To oversee the extensive area stretching to the Scottish border the king instituted a line of Norman prince-bishops. Rulers in both spiritual and temporal matters, they enjoyed full royal rights within the prince-bishopric or palatinate, possessing their own mint, exchequer, parliament, judiciary and army.

Stone carving of Bede, Jarrow

106

The city itself was to proclaim visually the authority and power of the new rulers of England. In so doing the evidence of Saxon beginnings was erased. A new castle was begun on the site of the old in 1072 at the vulnerable north neck of the peninsula, that being the only side not protected by the encircling river. A strong stone wall replaced wooden ramparts around the whole of the peninsula by the early 12th century. The Saxon 'White Church' was also erased and a new cathedral begun in 1093; this perhaps even more than the castle was a show of imperial force, its size and massive interior pillars suggesting it was indeed 'half castle 'gainst the Scot'. Its construction also incorporated stone ribbed vaulting for the roof, supported by concealed flying buttresses. As the first major building in the western world to do so, and as precursor of the Gothic, its place in architectural history was assured.

10th-century cross-head, Durham Cathedral

Associated with the cathedral arose a new abbey for a Benedictine monastic order which replaced the existing, more loosely organised community. The area between the cathedral and castle was cleared of housing on grounds of pollution and fire hazard, the population displaced being resettled at Framwellgate. Two bridges either side of the neck of the peninsula — Framwellgate (1128) to the small community on the west bank, and Elvet (1160) linking to the ancient borough of that name — complete the major components of Norman Durham. Collectively they have provided an indelible imprint.

Speed's map of 1610 clearly shows the Norman influence (Map 14). The formerly extra-mural market place is now incorporated within the city walls, the major roads winding their way from the two bridges and northwards along the Claypath spine. The general form at this time was quaintly likened by Robert Hegge to that of a crab, 'supposing the city for its belly and the suburbs for its claws'. The claws provided the links to the ancient churches of St Oswald (to the east of the peninsula), St Margaret (west) and St Giles (north) with their respective communities of Elvet, Crossgate with Framwellgate and Gilesgate. The fine detail of Speed's map permits an early glimpse of many features in the major buildings and defences of the city. Included in the latter are the various gates and fortified towers in the city wall, also the weirs, placed across the river to deepen the water for defensive purposes besides providing power for the mills.

During the intervening four centuries Durham had risen to its zenith in political and ecclesiastical prominence, a growth punctuated by skirmishes with the 'auld enemy', by periodic famine, and by the shock waves of the Reformation. A measure of its importance as a medieval centre is the number of visits to the city by royalty, mostly English but also, during peaceful interludes, by Scottish monarchs. The prince-bishops, in return for their privileges, had to maintain a fortified garrison

Laurence, 12th-century monk of Durham

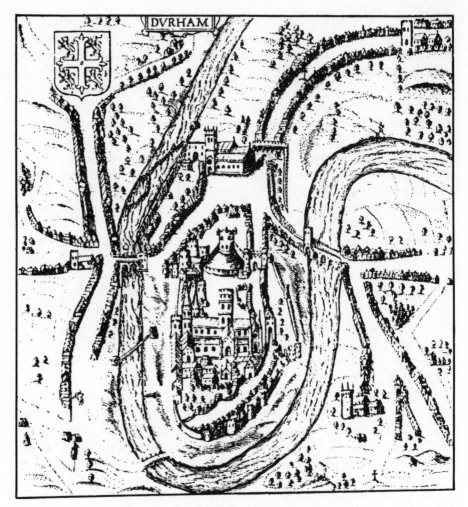

Map 14. Map of Durham by John Speed, 1610.

Monumental slab, St Oswald's, Durham

and fighting unit. The forces saw frequent action, both locally and further north. In 1346, for instance, with Edward III abroad, Bishop Neville helped to defeat the Scottish army in the western suburb now known as Neville's Cross. Or, again, at Flodden Field (1513) historians have the odd problem of whether to ascribe victory to the contribution of the bishop's army or to St Cuthbert's banner specially carried for the campaign.

The reputation and splendour of the cathedral of St Cuthbert with its associated abbey meant that the city was an ecclesiastical focus of England. The transfer of the endowments of Jarrow and Monkwearmouth, gifts from early Norman bishops, and the general Benedictine

108

42. Prominent 20th-century personalities in County Durham:

(a) Peter Lee.

(b) Ellen Wilkinson, M.P.

(c) Thomas Sharp.

43. The Jarrow Crusade, 1936. Two hundred men on their march to London to deliver a petition to the House of Commons.

44. Whitton Park. This slum housing was a category 'D' settlement.

45. Team Valley Trading Estate, Gateshead, 1939. Designed by William Holford in 1936, it was the first trading estate in the country.

46. Washington New Town, designed 'to cater for full motorisation'.

47. Opencast coal working at Ibbotson's Syke in the mid-1970s. The honeycomb of pillars and stalls from earlier conventional mining has been exposed.

48. Sunderland, looking downriver to Monkwearmouth colliery (left), and the site of Lambton Drops in the distance.

49. Sherburn Hill Colliery spoil heap before reclamation.

50. The same view after County Council restoration.

emphasis on education and learning ensured that Durham was the intellectual centre of the North. Its manuscripts included the Lindisfarne Gospels; its foundations included Durham College (later Trinity College), Oxford, where brothers were sent to complete their studies. Scholars, however, were far outnumbered by pilgrims flocking to a cathedral which contained not only the elaborate shrines of St Cuthbert and Bede, and the head of a second northern saint, Oswald, but also a supporting assortment of holy relics.

Shell-hood to doorway, South Bailey, Durham

The splendour of ecclesiastical Durham was trimmed by the Reformation, but fortunately the foundation remained, so that continuity as well as change was evident. The cathedral was stripped of its shrines, relics and other embellishments — and also of its dedication to St Cuthbert— but not of its bishop. The abbey was dissolved by Henry VIII, but it was a peaceful transition. The buildings remained intact, while the abbey prior was successfully translated into a dean and 12 monks became cathedral prebendaries or canons. If anything the changes had a greater impact on the city, which, always subservient to the bishop, lost much of the trade connected with pilgrims, festivals and fairs.

After another two centuries — including the disturbed period of the Commonwealth when the bishopric was temporarily abolished and the dean and chapter suppressed — the next period of significance in forming the character of the city was the 18th century. It was an era which became increasingly noted for its architectural and landscape elegance.

Georgian structures — more often reconstructions — graced the College and the Baileys on the peninsula, in Old Elvet and South Street. The residences in the College, the former abbey site, housed the so-called 'golden canons', renowned for being among the richest in the country. Along the Baileys, on the site of premises originally occupied by the bishop's military tenants or barons, there were new town houses for county families. Their gardens extended to the old city wall before forming hanging gardens down to the river. Life was certainly gracious for those at the top, and Durham, still over a week's journey distant from London, was now a sophisticated county town and cultural centre. In the season the citizen might attend horse racing, go to the theatre, dance or play cards in the Assembly Rooms, entertain or just promenade.

Promenading became increasingly fashionable with the emergence of the English taste for the picturesque, for 'composed' landscape. From this period, then, stemmed the active landscape gardening of the river banks by the dean and chapter. Previously the slopes below the cathedral and castle in particular had been bare — and known as 'Bishop's Waste' — but now an active programme of planting and path-making sought to produce a series of contrived vistas. After visiting it, the poet Thomas Gray wrote that he had discovered 'one of the most beautiful

Old Elvet Bridge, with chapel of St Andrew, Durham

City of Durham arms

Vales in England to walk in with prospects that change every ten steps, and open up something new wherever I turn me, all rude and romantic'. A visual climax was provided in 1778 when a new Prebends' Bridge, paid for by the prebendaries and named after them, replaced a more modest construction that had been destroyed by floods. Positioned some 50 yards downstream from the old crossing, the new bridge was clear of the meander loop and so revealed the classic prospect of gorge and citadel.

Notable as a county town, Durham developed little manufacturing industry, although it did claim the first commercial production of mustard in the world in 1720. There is nothing to suppose that more would have arisen had any of the four schemes to make the Wear navigable from Durham to its mouth and to the Tyne come to pass, for a new form of locomotion was about to arise which, in association with the rapidly increasing exploitation of coal, was to change the face of the county and encourage development elsewhere.

Although 19th-century County Durham possessed the country's most productive coalfield and saw the birth of rail transport, the county town remained largely unaffected by the industrial expansion of the age. The coal seams under the centre of the city were generally too thin for large-scale economic exploitation, while lack of interest as much as opposition accounted for the late and circuitous connection to the rail network. Moreover, lack of suitable level sites and of water transport put Durham at a disadvantage compared with many centres. Population figures summarise the consequent shift in fortune: in 1801 its population total of 7,500 had only recently conceded first place in the county to Sunderland; by the end of the century the county figure had increased tenfold and the county town (although it had reached 16,000) had slipped to twelfth position. Industrial-urban growth along the river-estuaries of the Tyne and Tees across the county boundary put its regional ranking in even poorer light.

The unenthusiastic response to industrial development meant that Durham did not undergo the marked character change typical of so many English towns. A dozen or so streets of bye-law housing to the west of the peninsula — they provide the rail passenger's vista of the cathedral — suggest what might have been, but topography, if not land-ownership, prevented any emergence of a Victorian collar to the central core. Apart from organ construction and a carpet factory, local initiatives which have grown to serve world-wide markets, Durham's manufactures were those of a small county town serving itself and a restricted hinterland, destined for eclipse as technological advance favoured specialised centres. Such activities were corn and paper milling, brewing and malting, iron and brass founding, worsted spinning and wool combing.

University of Durham arms

110

Rather than become an industrial centre, Durham found it more natural to foster the creation of England's third university. Mooted in the 16th century, actually sanctioned in the 17th, the institution finally came to fruition in 1832 on the initiative of the dean and chapter and bishop who provided both income and accommodation, the latter including several buildings on Palace Green, not least the bishop's palace — the castle — in 1837. Bishop van Mildert piloted the Durham University Bill through parliament. He was the last of the prince-bishops; his initiative with regard to a university deflected possible confiscation of revenues from the see of Durham in the imminent Reform Bill. The timing also coincided with rumours of universities in other provincial cities. From the point of view of townscape, the decision of 1832 was a stabilising influence, ensuring respect for the buildings initially possessed and for those subsequently acquired or commissioned.

Monument to Bishop Van Mildert

Besides removal of the bishop's residence (to Bishop Auckland), other institutions to leave the peninsula for new locations were the public school (to an extensive green site on church land on the other side of Prebends' Bridge, 1844), the gaol, with the assize court (to Old Elvet), and the County Hospital (to the western fringe of the city in 1860).

The changing structures and powers of local government wrought other significant and permanent changes on the face of Durham during the 19th century. The Market Place was reshaped in the 1850s. The west side had a new town hall and associated market building; the north side was filled by a rebuilt St Nicholas church; while diagonally opposite two banks contributed further dignity to the square. County links, of which the prominent equestrian statue of Lord Londonderry in the Market Place and the miners' headquarters in a new North Road provided contrasting symbols, were formalised by a large Shire Hall in Old Elvet. But the construction which perhaps best symbolises the century in Durham is the multi-arched and curving railway viaduct. Its lofty but peripheral position symbolises how 19th-century industrial power was so near, yet passed by the town. The viaduct was not built until 1857, and not until 1872 was there a direct link between London and Newcastle. A branch line had reached the end of Gilesgate in 1844 but remained isolated and unimportant; another feeder line reached the head of Old Elvet in 1897 but was even more local and insignificant.

The present century has seen much change in the Durham scene. In terms of population growth, however, there was a long pause between the two world wars: the 1951 census figure of 19,000 was no higher than that for 1921. The inter-war decline in the county's basic industries and general era of economic and social depression was no springboard for growth in the county town. But that did not prevent the beginning of several significant structural changes. Clearance of slum property near

St Nicholas' church, Durham

111

Kepier Hospital gateway

the waterside in Framwellgate, with resettlement of the displaced community on the plateau rim to the north-east at Gilesgate in the 1930s, was a centrifugal process observable also in the university, with its first building to the south of the river in 1924, and the hospital moving to its extensive northern site in 1942. Along the western ridge a sequence of roads, soon quickly lined with ribbon development, was linked to form a new Great North Road through Neville's Cross, thus bypassing the central city for the first time.

During the most recent era of growth the census population figure had reached 25,000 by 1974, when local government reorganisation redrew the map of the county, dividing it into eight districts, with the central one incorporating and taking the name of 'City of Durham'. By this time the boundaries of the old municipal borough had been breached on all but the south side. A coherent urban entity, containing some 35,000 of the new district's 80,000 total, had emerged through extensive residential development on the surrounding plateaux, especially to the north and east. From the townscape point of view, this development is significantly beyond the rim of the central basin, in the middle of which is the cathedral on the raised peninsula. Since the rim, at three-quarters of a mile from the centre, has been largely spared from development, the experience when in the historic core remains that of being in a small city. (Plate 16 is an aerial view of the centre.) In reality, beyond the rim are found not only residential estates, but industrial estates and a new prison. Nearer, but concealed by folds in the rolling topography north of the centre are a new county hall, land registry, museum and hospital. The equivalent rising land to the south has been studded by university buildings.

The route of the Great North Road has been changed again, being transferred to the east of the city and given motorway status. The connecting dual-carriageway link, built over the line of the branch railway to Gilesgate and seemingly aimed at the very heart of the city, highlights the threat which increasing traffic posed to the enclosed core. The solution adopted in 1967 was to use the southward-facing slope of the Claypath ridge to lead to two new bridges across the Wear at either end of the northern neck of the peninsula (Map 15). The first connects with New Elvet, the second, after tunnelling under Claypath, crosses the river fresh from its meander loop and enters North Road. This scheme opened up another scenic entry to the city, but the Claypath underpass, necessitating removal of properties overhead, breached not only the physical neck of the peninsula but also the urban fabric, opening up the formerly enclosed Market Place. Across the river, road alignment incurred demolition of some property only recently erected, although a much more controversial feature was the decision to locate

Durham Cathedral
postal frank

112

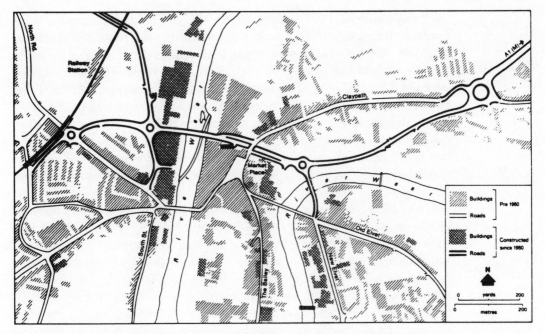

Map 15. The new inner road system in Durham.

the largest building to be erected in the city for 800 years, the National Savings Certificate Office, adjacent to the bridge on the west bank.

The new road system relieved the central medieval streets of vehicular traffic (or largely so, for the river-girt peninsula precludes any extensive rear-serving of premises, commercial or otherwise). Following this key step, the Market Place and narrow streets have been resurfaced in stone and many facades of properties rejuvenated by sand-blasting or painted according to a co-ordinated colour scheme. The planning authority has been able to encourage general building restoration through control and grants available in listed building and conservation area legislation. The conservation area was designated in 1968, one of the earliest in England, and has recently been extended. Good husbandry has been further facilitated in that the two largest property-owners are the Church and the university, the latter now with much old property in Elvet as well as on the peninsula.

The attention in this chapter devoted to the physical and built environment witnesses to a city of distinctive quality. That distinctiveness is conveyed by an air of apartness, even aloofness: of being in, but not of, the area. In the very beginning, for instance, the city did not evolve out of a relationship with the surrounding countryside; it was planted

Cathedral arms

113

by Saxon pilgrims and confirmed by the conquering Normans, who made it the political and ecclesiastical centre for much of northern England. After centuries of only moderate pretence as a market centre, the city remained aloof from the industrial revolution and almost unscarred by coal-mining despite being in the geographical centre of the extensive coalfield. At the peak of landscape disfigurement Thomas Sharp described the remarkable contrast in the terms of the cathedral city being 'a flower among the filth'. This apparent aloofness of the city did not mean lack of involvement, however, for many of the colliery leases were on dean and chapter estates from which considerable revenue accrued.

Other factors have compounded the characteristic of being in, but not of, the area. The university, for instance, is decidedly national, rather than local or provincial in character and orientation. A perceived reluctance to turn the distinguished microscope of scholarship on its home area caused local writer Sid Chaplin to refer to the students and teachers as 'colonialists' and to the institution as 'stuck in the county's crop'. Again, the largest single success by local government to encourage post-war employment was not home-grown but the National Savings Unit, decentralised as part of central government policy from London. The city's employment structure as a whole is quite unrepresentative of the region in which it is set. The area over which administration is exercised may well have contracted since its Norman foundation, but the complexity of our bureaucratic society is such that Durham is the headquarters for many services provided not only on a county basis but also on a regional level. The character of the city is influenced accordingly and is set apart in any table of averages, be they economic, social or political. But it is the consequent urban response that remains the most tangible sign of apartness. Offering one of the architectural experiences of Europe, the city may be said to 'belong' to the nation rather than to the local area. Indeed, the designation of the cathedral and castle as a World Heritage Site in 1987 was the ultimate confirmation of its value and distinctiveness. Aesthetically and architecturally, historically and culturally, therefore, it is a fitting climax on which to conclude our study.

Dun Cow carving on Cathedral, c.1800

Further Reading

Allen, C. J., *The North Eastern Railway* (London, Allan, 1964).

Allibone, J., *Anthony Salvin, Pioneer of Gothic Revival Architecture* (Cambridge, Lutterworth Press, 1988).

Atkinson, F., *The Great Northern Coalfield 1700-1900* (London, University Tutorial Press, 1968).

Atkinson, F., *The Industrial Archaeology of the North East*. 2 vols. (Newton Abbot, David and Charles, 1974).

Atkinson, F., *North East England: People at Work, 1860-1950* (Moorland Publishing, 1980).

Austin, D. (ed.), *Boldon Book: Northumberland and Durham* (Chichester, Phillimore, 1982).

Bailey, J., *General View of the Agriculture of County Durham* (London, 1810).

Beadle, H. L., 'Mining and Smelting in Teesdale', *Research Report no. 3* (Cleveland Industrial Archaeology Society, 1980).

Bede, trans. L. Sherley-Price, rev. R. E. Latham, *A History of the English Church and People* (Harmondsworth, Penguin Books, 1968).

Bell, T. G., 'Report on the Agriculture of County Durham', *Journal of Royal Agricultural Society*, vol. 17, pp.86-123 (1856).

Billings, R. W., *Illustrations of the Architectural Antiquities of the County of Durham* (1846, facsimile reprint 1974).

Blair, P. H., *Northumbria in the Days of Bede* (London, Gollancz, 1976).

Bonner, G. I., *Famulus Christi: Essays in Commemoration of the 13th Centenary of the Birth of the Venerable Bede* (London, S.P.C.K., 1976).

Bonner, G., Rollason, D. and Stancliffe, C. (eds.), *St Cuthbert, his Cult and Community to A.D.1200* (Woodbridge, Boydell, 1989).

Bonney, M., *Lordship and the Urban Community: Durham and its Overlord, 1250-1510* (Cambridge, Cambridge University Press, 1990).

Brunskill, R. W., 'Vernacular architecture of the Northern Pennines', *Northern History*, vol. 11, pp.107-42 (1976).

Bulmer, M. I. A. (ed.), *Mining and Social Change: Durham County in the 20th Century* (London, Croom-Helm, 1978).

Chapman, J. C. and Mytum, M. C. (eds.), *Settlement in North Britain, 1000 B.C.-1000 A.D.* (London, British Archaeological Reports, International Series, no. 118).

Clack, P., *The Book of Durham City* (Buckingham, Barracuda, 1985).

Clack, P. and Gosling, P. F. (eds.), *Archaeology in the North* (London, H.M.S.O., 1976).

Clapham, A. R. (ed.), *Upper Teesdale: The Area and its Natural History* (London, Collins, 1978).

Clarke, C. W., *Farewell Squalor: A Design for a New Town and Proposals for the Redevelopment of Easington Rural District* (West Hartlepool, Easington Rural District, 1946).

Coggins, D. and Fairless, K. J., 'The Bronze Age settlement of Bracken Rigg, Upper Teesdale, Co. Durham', *Durham Archaeological Journal*, no. 1, pp.5-22 (1984).

Corfe, T., *Sunderland: A Short History* (Newcastle, Frank Graham, 1973).

Cramp, R., 'Anglo-Saxon monasteries of the North', *Scottish Archaeological Forum*, no. 5 (1973).

Crosby, J. H., *Ignatius Bonomi of Durham, Architect* (Tudhoe, City of Durham Trust, 1987).

Daysh, G. H. J. and Symonds, J. S., *West Durham* (Oxford, Oxford University Press, 1953).

Coat of arms,
Bishop Antony
Bek (1284-1311)

115

Dewdney, J. C. (ed.), *Durham County and City with Teesside* (Durham, British Association, 1970).

Dickinson, P. and Fisher, W. B., *The Medieval Land Surveys of County Durham* (Dept. of Geography, University of Durham, Research Paper Series no. 2, 1959).

Dougan, D. J., *The History of North East Shipbuilding* (London, Allen and Unwin, 1968).

Durham County Council, *County Development Plan, Draft Written Analysis* (Durham, 1951).

Durham County Council, *County Development Plan, Amendment* (Durham, 1964).

Durham County Council, *County Structure Plan* (Durham, 1981).

Durham County Council, *The Durham Book* (Durham, 1982).

Durham County Council, *Lead and Life at Killhope* (Durham, 1987).

Eden, Sir T. C., *Durham*, 2 vols. (London, Robert Hale, 1952).

Farmer, D. H. (ed.), *The Age of Bede* (Harmondsworth, Penguin Books, 1983).

Fordyce, W., *The History and Antiquities of the County Palatine of Durham* (Newcastle, T. Fordyce, 1857).

Garside, W. R., *The Durham Miners, 1919-1960* (London, Allen and Unwin, 1971).

Granger, J., *General View of the Agriculture of the County of Durham* (London, Macrae, 1794).

Hair, T., *Sketches of the Coal Mines in Northumberland and Durham* (London, James Madden and Co., 1844).

Harding, A. F. and Young, R., 'Pictures of an exhibition: new discoveries concerning the Heathery Burn hoard', *Durham Archaeological Journal*, vol. 2, pp. 1-5 (1986).

Heesom, A., 'The enfranchisement of Durham', *Durham University Journal*, vol. 80, pp. 268-85 (1988).

Higham, N., *The Northern Counties to A.D. 1000* (London, Longman, 1986).

Hodgson, R. I., 'The progress of enclosure in County Durham, 1550-1870', in H. S. A. Fox and R. A. Butlin (eds.), *Change in the Countryside: Essays on Rural England, 1550-1900* (Institute of British Geographers, Special Publication no. 10, pp.83-102, 1979).

Hoole, K., *A Regional History of the Railways of Great Britain, vol. 4, North East England* (Dawlish, David and Charles, 1965).

House, J. W., *Industrial Britain: The North East* (Newton Abbot, David and Charles, 1969).

Hughes, E., *North Country Life in the Eighteenth Century: The North East 1700-1750* (London, University of Durham, 1952).

Hutchinson, W., *The History and Antiquities of the County Palatine of Durham*, 3 vols. (Newcastle, S. Hodgson, 1785-1794).

James, M., *Family, Lineage and Civil Society: A Study of Society, Politics and Mentality in the Durham Region 1500-1640* (Oxford, Oxford University Press, 1974).

Jobey, G., Clack, P. and Haselgrove, S. (eds.), *Rural Settlement in the Roman North* (Durham, Council for British Archaeology, Group 3, 1981).

Johnson, F. F., *Historic Staircases in Durham City* (Durham, City of Durham Trust, 1970).

Lapsley, G. T., *The County Palatine of Durham: A Study in Constitutional History* (New York, University of Harvard, 1900).

Leister, I., *The Sea-Coal Mine and the Durham Miner* (Dept. of Geography, University of Durham, Occasional Paper no. 5, 1975).

McCord, N., *North East England: An Economic and Social History* (London, Batsford, 1979).

McCord, N. and Rowe, D. J., *Northumberland and Durham: Industry in the Nineteenth Century* (Newcastle, Frank Graham, 1971).

Marcombe, D. (ed.), *The Last Principality: Politics, Religion and Society in the Bishopric of Durham, 1494-1660* (Nottingham, University of Nottingham, 1987).

Miket, R., *The Prehistory of Tyne and Wear* (Gateshead, Northumberland Archaeological Group, 1984).

Moore, R. S., *Pitmen, Preachers and Politics* (Cambridge, Cambridge University Press, 1974).

Morris, C. D., 'Northumbrian and Viking settlement: the evidence for land-holding', *Archaeologia Aeliana*, vol. 5, pp.81-104 (1977).

Moyes, W. A., *Mostly Mining* (Newcastle, Frank Graham, 1969).

Moyes, W. A., *Contracting Coalfield* (Newcastle, Frank Graham, 1971).

Northern Architect, no. 6 (September 1962); no. 47 (July 1969).

The North East: A Programme for Regional Development and Growth ('The Hailsham Report'), Cmd. 2206 (London, H.M.S.O., 1963).

Page, W. (ed.), *Victoria County History: Durham*, 3 vols. (London, Archibald Constable, 1905-28).

Pevsner, N., *The Buildings of England: County Durham* (Harmondsworth, Penguin Books, 1953, rev. 1983).

Philipson, G., *Aycliffe and Peterlee New Towns, 1946-1988* (Cambridge Publication for Companies, 1988).

Pocock, D., *A Mining World* (Durham, City of Durham Trust, 1986).

Pocock, D. and Gazzard, R., *Durham: Portrait of a Cathedral City* (Dept. of Geography, University of Durham,1983).

Raistrick, A. and Jennings, R., *A History of Lead Mining in the Pennines* (London, Longmans, 1965).

Roberts, B. K., *The Green Villages of County Durham: A study in Historical Geography* (Durham, Durham County Library Local History Publication, 1977).

Rollason, D. W. and Bonner, G. I., *Cuthbert, Saint and Patron* (Durham, Dean and Chapter, 1987).

Scott, P. R., 'The bridges at Piercebridge, County Durham: a reassessment', *Transactions of the Architectural and Archaeological Society of Durham and Northumberland*, no. 6, pp.77-82 (1982).

Sedman, K. W., *The Mines and Minerals of Teesdale and Weardale* (Middlesbrough, Cleveland County Museum Service, 1987).

Selkirk, P., *The Piercebridge Formula* (Cambridge, Cambridge University Press, 1982).

Sharp, T., *A Derelict Area: A Study of the South-West Durham Coalfield* (London, Day to Day Pamphlets no. 25, 1935).

Sharp, T., 'The North-East: Hills and Hells' in C. Williams-Ellis, ed., *Britain and the Beast* (London, J. M. Dent and Sons, 1938).

Sharp, T., *Cathedral City: A Plan for Durham* (London, Architectural Press, 1945).

Shranks, C. J., *This Sumptuous Church: The Story of Durham Cathedral* (London, S.P.C.K., 1973).

Smailes, A. E., *North England* (London, Nelson and Sons, 1960).

Still, L. and Vyner, B. E., 'Air photograph evidence for later prehistoric settlement in the Tees valley', *Durham Archaeological Journal*, vol. 2, pp.11-23 (1986).

Sturgess, R. W., *The Great Age of Industry in the North East, 1700-1920* (Durham, Durham County Local History Society, 1981).

Surtees, R., *The History and Antiquities of the County Palatine of Durham*, 4 vols. (London, 1816-40).

Thompson, H., *Durham Villages* (London, Hale, 1976).

Thorold, H., *County Durham* (London, Faber, 1980).

Thorpe, H., 'The Green Villages of County Durham', *Transactions of the Institute of British Geographers*, no. 15, pp.155-80 (1949).

Vernon, B. D., *Ellen Wilkinson, 1891-1947* (London, Croom-Helm, 1982).

Waggott, E., *Jackson's Town* (Hartlepool, Hartlepool Borough Corporation, 1980).

Whiting, C. E., *The University of Durham 1832-1932* (London, University of Durham, 1932).

Whittaker, N. and Clark, V., *Historic Architecture of County Durham* (Newcastle, Oriel Press, 1971).

Wilcock, D., *The Durham Coalfield — 1: The 'Sea Coal Age'* (Durham, Durham County Library Local History Publication, 1979).

Wood, R., *West Hartlepool: The Rise and Development of a Victorian New Town* (West Hartlepool Corporation, 1967).

Young, A., *A Six Months Tour through the North of England* (London, Straham, 1770).

Young, R., 'An inventory of barrows in County Durham', *Transactions of the Architectural and Archaeological Society of Durham and Northumberland*, New Series, no. 5, pp.1-16 (1980).

Coat of arms,
Bishop Thomas of
Hatfield (1345-81)

117

Index

*Coat of arms,
Bishop Robert
Neville (1438-57)*

119

Coat of arms,
Bishop Van Mildert
(1826-36)

South-west view of Durham City, from Greenwood's *Map of the County Palatine of Durham*, 1820.